FLIGHT TRAINING TO AIRLINE PILOT

What every potential pilot needs to know about the aviation industry

Title: Flight Training To Airline Pilot 3rd edition

Author: Williams, Robert

ISBN: 978-0-244-26692-9

"Pilots take no special joy in walking. Pilots like flying"

Neil Armstrong

CONTENTS

Flying training

Your first job

After your first job

1

The purpose of this book was to assist potential pilots looking at obtaining a job within the Australian aviation industry. Aviation is a very difficult and expensive industry to "break" into. Unfortunately, it is not until someone has spent a fair amount of time, and thus money that one can start to identify how this particular industry operates. There are many different paths that one may choose to becoming an airline pilot including instructing, general aviation, parachuting, Defence Force and in more recent times, through the prevalence of cadetships straight into an airline. On any of these paths however, attempting to plan a career without having the experience can prove costly.

Although catering for anyone looking at obtaining a pilots licence, regardless of aspirations, this guide was written primarily for those whom were entering general aviation and building their hours through that avenue. In more recent times however, there has been a push towards cadet programs to source pilots to support airlines, especially with Virgin Australia and Qantas advertising increasing pilot opportunities throughout 2020 and beyond.

This additional update to the book focuses on the changes to the industry since then, and helps build on the pertinent information that wil
applying for a position with an airline, particularly as a cadet.

Every week we hear about the looming pilot shortage and the simple fact that we do not currently have enough qualified pilots throughout Australia and the world to sustain the explosion in air travel over the near future. Boeing, one of the largest aircraft manufacturers in the world, has published a report stating that over the next 20 years, there will be a worldwide demand for an additional 790,000 pilots. Of that 790,000 261,000 are estimated to be required in the Asia/Pacific region which includes Australia.

Now more than ever has it been the perfect time to consider a career as a pilot in the aviation industry. Under our current training avenues in Australia, sustainability of this type of grown is not possible. Both Qantas and Virgin Australia know this and have been proactive by announcing they will be setting up Cadetship training schools throughout the country which will be able to train aspiring pilots from zero hours right through to being an operationally ready First or Second Officer within their respective company.

Qantas have begun to set up their training facility at Wellcamp West Toowoomba airport in Queensland whilst Virgin Australia, in association with Flight Training Adelaide (FTA), will base a cadet training school at Tamworth Airport in New South Wales.

In addition, Virgin Australia has set themselves the ambitious goal of a 50/50 gender split for pilots entering Virgin Australia through the cadet program.

Although both Qantas and Virgin Australia will still hire direct entry pilots who have gained experience through General Aviation, which was the main discussion of this book, it seems that cadetships are a major avenue for both airlines to hire the necessary pilots in the future.

For this reason, it was pertinent to include an update to the second edition of the book. This update which makes this the 3rd edition of this book, will flesh out more details in regards to cadet programs, and gives important information to any aspiring pilot whom wishes to seek a position within the airlines, whether Qantas, Virgin, Tiger, Jetstar or others.

Just a final note. It has taken a tremendous amount of time to write and format this book. Please do not copy or send this book to anyone else. For the cost of a few cups of coffee, I would appreciate if you keep the information to yourself, and tell your friends whom may be interested in buying the book to head over to www.australian-pilot.com to purchase the book themselves. As an appreciation, they can use the coupon code *REFERRAL* to get 10% off the price of the book.

Virgin Australian Cadetship

Virgin Australia was previously offering two types of cadetships; ab-initio and advanced. The ab-initio course is designed to train a successful applicant from zero hours right up to the qualifications necessary to be employed either as a Second Officer on the Virgin Australia Long Haul operation on the Boeing 777-300ER or as a First Officer with *Virgin Australia* on the ATR-72 600. In 2019, the direct entry cadetship was scrapped so now the ab-initio cadet program will be the only cadetship offered. (The direct entry minimum requirements have been reduced which means that the advanced cadetship has become obsolete).

Minimum requirements

The minimum requirements for the *Virgin Australia* cadetship for 2019 (at the time of writing) are the following:

- ✈ Minimum age of 18 years
- ✈ Australian Citizen or Permanent Resident
- ✈ Passport holder with a minimum of 18 months validity
- ✈ Completion of High School with high level achievements in the Sciences (preferably Physics), Advanced Maths and English (if these subjects were not undertaken at school, an equivalent bridging course with high level achievements must have been completed)
- ✈ Ability to successfully obtain an ASIC (Aviation Security Identification Card)
- ✈ No flying experience required however training up to a PPL is okay.

Application and selection process

The first stage of applying for the *Virgin Australia* Cadetship is by applying through the careers page on the *Virgin Australia* website. You will then be asked to conduct a video interview which can be completed from home.

The next stage will be to conduct psychometric testing through *Aviation Australia* which is located directly opposite from the *Virgin Australia* simulator Center at Brisbane airport.

If successful, the following day, candidates will be asked to attend an interview and group panel assessment. The panel consists of Human Resource employees as well as current *Virgin Australia* pilots whom work within recruitment. The interview is behavioral based whereby you will be asked approximately 6-8 questions relating to previous life and job experiences and how you dealt with those situations. These questions normally start with "tell us about a time..." whereby you then have to explain a past experience and how you handled it. Example questions include situations such as:

"Tell us about a time you saved the day"

"Tell us about a time you had to work to a deadline and how you managed your time effectively"

"Tell us about a time you had to deal with someone difficult and how you handled the situation"

"Tell us about a time you turned a negative situation into a positive one"

These types of behavioral questions are based on the premise that how you dealt with a situation in the past can be a good indicator of how you would handle a similar situation in the future. There is more information on behavioral interviews later in this book.

The group exteriors focuses on. A particular situation, which as a group of prospective employees, must deal with and work together to achieve a positive outcome. Virgin Australia staff are looking at how you interact with fellow candidates and how you conduct yourself, communicate and work together.

Training

At the time of writing, the cadet program in 2019 will still be completed in Adelaide through *Flight Training Adelaide* (FTA). The cadet program runs for approximately one year, with cadets living onsite at Parafield airport, learning together with fellow pilots.

Upon successful completion of the training program, *Virgin Australia* guarantees a permanent position with the airline as a pilot, assuming that the cadet also meets and successfully completes *Virgin Australia* specific training, such as ATR or 777 type rating, Dangerous Goods, Security Training, Emergency Procedures training, terms of employment and any other related courses that are required.

Qantas Cadetship

Qantas is beginning the Qantas Group Pilot Academy in 2019 with the academy expected to open its door in 2019 for highschool and university graduate with strong academic performance.

The initial intake for the program will be 100 pilots. Once the academy is setup, *Qantas* is expecting to train up to 500 pilots per annum. Pilots can register their interest for the cadetship for 2019 through the Qantas website.

Although minimum requirements have not yet been established, you can expect that they'd be very similar to the *Virgin Australia* minimum requirements listed on the previous page.

The Qantas Group contains all airlines, not just Qantas mainline. It consists of *Qantas, Qantaslink, Jetstar, Network Aviation*, and *Jetconnect*. Once finished training, Qantas expects that its cadets will move to different parts of the Qantas Group such as Jetstar and Qantaslink.

Application and selection process

Applying for and being selected by *Qantas* is quite a lengthy process. The process outlined here is the same, regardless of cadet or direct entry applications.

The first step is applying via their website. The application portal can "grab" some of the information it requires should you wish to sign in via Facebook or Google. I would recommend being wary of using any social media account to sign into a prospective employer application portal and suggest that you fill in the information manually - even if only for the reason of knowing that the information you are providing is up to date.

The process will ask you to upload a resume/CV. A good tip would be write a cover letter and make this the first page of your resume, so that it is the same PDF/DOC file, so that when *Qantas* HR opens up your attached file, the first page of your resume would be your covering letter which would introduce your resume.

You will receive an automated email advising that your application has been received. The first step in the selection process is an online psychometric/behaviour test (*TalentQ*) which is split into different categories. Conducted at home in front of your computer. The first portion is time and based on numerical, verbal and logical reasoning, while the second portion is an approximately 200 question behaviour questionnaire with no time limit.

If successful candidates will be required to attend an initial assessment day at the *Qantas* Jet Base in Mascot, Sydney.

On day 1, the first assessment is a group exercise. Conducted in groups of 4 candidates and is assessed by 2 human resources employees and 1 pilot. The aim of the group exercise is to work as a team and you will be assessed in how you interact and communicate. The group exercise is not based on obtaining the correct answer, however rather how you work together to solve a problem. An example situation they might pose is that a *Qantas* A330 has diverted to an alternate aerodrome out of Singapore with 200 passengers on board. There are no ground staff at the diversion aerodrome and you will be asked how you would manage the situation. It is a time based exercise, where you will have 15 minutes total – 5 minutes to write down any considerations and then 5-10 minutes to talk amongst yourselves. After you have answered this, you will be asked a second part of the question which could be along the lines of, once all passengers have been disembarked, the plane will then need to be ferried back to Singapore, so how would you organize this and which crew/passengers would you take.

Once you have completed the group exercise, the second component of the day will be the behavioural questionnaire consisting of 557 true or false questions. The time limit for the questionnaire is 90 minutes and consists of questions such as "I hear thoughts in my head", "I've drunk excessive alcohol before", "do you like fire, or do you think fire is scary". The key is to work somewhat quickly through the questions so you don't second guess your first answer that comes to mind. Be careful however of double negative, contained within some of the questions.

A lunch break will be provided at this stage, with the next assessment after being a revalidation of the *TalentQ* behavioural test. You will be required to answer 3 questions from each category of numerical, verbal and logical reasoning. The validation is to ensure that no external help was used during the testing completed at home and you meet the benchmark.

Once this has been completed, you will then conduct the interview. The interview is done in front of a panel of a human resources employee and one pilot. Apart from the behavioral questions, you will be asked 3 specific questions which include "Tell us about yourself", "Why do you want to work for *Qantas*" and "What challenges has *Qantas* previously faced and in the future". More details on how to answer behavioural based questions is given in chapter 8.

Finally, on day 1, you will need to answer a few scenario based questions. These are done individually in front of an assessor. Some typical scenarios might include situations such as, departing Sydney on the 737 as Pilot in command, the cargo door won't close and engineering is half an hour away. What would you do, in what sequence and why? You will be given 15 minutes to think about an answer and write it down before presenting your ideas.

After you have explained what you would do in that situation, you will be given part 2 of the scenario which will continue on from the same example, such as, engineering can't fix the door, the passengers are getting disruptive and the on-board leader is trying to deal with the situation. Another 737 is about to depart but can only carry half of your passengers, what are you going to do and why?

Second day consists of a simulator flight test in the Boeing 767. Conducted out of Melbourne, you will be required to takeoff, accelerate, level off, conduct turns and steep turns onto specified headings, an ILS, go-around, intercept a certain radial from the ML VOR and then conduct a LOC NPA. All conducted on runway 16 with no flight directors. You will also be asked to conduct engine failures, crosswind takeoffs and landings.

Once completed, the next stage will be to conduct a Qantas medical. These can be done in specific capital cities around Australia. At the time of writing, the out of pocket expense for the medical is approximately $1000.

A reference check will then be completed and finally, your file will then be presented to the executive board which will review all applications whom have passed all stages of the process. From there, your application will either be deemed successful or unsuccessful. *Qantas* will then offer a full time position or alternatively, you will be placed on a hold file which means you have been successful in your interview, however there currently no vacancies and you will be placed in a pool of pilots to be offered a position in the future.

Regional Express (REX) Cadetship

REX is offering positions within its cadet program where training will be conducted by the *Australian Airline Pilot Academy* (AAPA) in Wagga Wagga, New South Wales which is a wholly owned subsidiary of *REX*.

As with the *Virgin Australia* program, cadets will live onsite for approximately 34 weeks, living with fellow pilots who are also training.

Application and selection process

Applying for the *REX* Cadetship is quite a lengthy process. The first step of applying for the *REX* Cadetship is by submitting a cover letter and resume/CV. The *REX* website states that this must include all contact details, secondary and any tertiary qualifications, previous work experience, whether aviation related or not and total flying hours (if applicable). If you have a logbook, CASA medical or ASIC these will also need to be sighted.

In a separate email, you'll have to attach all supporting documentation as the application portal size limit for uploads is very small. It would be wise to update your CV and application at least every six months.

If you are successful, candidates will be asked to sit what is called a "WOMBAT" test which runs for approximately 2 and a half hours. The *REX* website also states that some applicants may have to sit a math and physics test on the same day - you will be told before the day whether this will be required however. If there are any gaps in your education etc, they may ask you to do this. To be proactive, you can inform them via the phone call when you first speak to them that you're willing to do the physics and math test.

More details on the WOMBAT test as well as a PDF which details exactly what is covered is available from the website www.aapa.net.au/programmes-CADET.html. The WOMBAT test covers hand eye coordination, situation awareness and stress testing.

Something to be aware of is that the test is quite old using very old equipment and computers. Some candidates have reported that the bottom of the screen which contains the progress bar can sometimes be cut off by the monitor and that the test may freeze on occasion. Knowing this beforehand will help you be aware of this fact in case this occurs.

If successful in the WOMBAT test, the next stage is an interview which is conducted over the phone. If successful for the phone interview, you will be asked to attend a panel interview in Wagga Wagga. If successful with the interview, candidates will immediately (on the same day) have to conduct a simulator flight test which covers basic flying skills over the course of half an hour.

If successful, candidates will be shortlisted for an interview in front of a selection committee conducted by *REX* management in Sydney.

The final stage of the process is to write a letter which must be hand written, explaining why you would like to work for *REX*, explain your reasoning for wanting to be a cadet for REX, show your passion for aviation and discuss what the *REX* Cadetship would mean for you personally.

Training

Upon successful completion of the training program, *REX* guarantees a permanent position with the airline as a pilot, assuming that the cadet also meets and successfully completes *REX* specific training, such as Dangerous Goods, Security Training, Emergency Procedures training, terms of employment and any other related courses that are required.

It can take a lot of perseverance obtaining a job in the aviation industry, but it's definitely worth it. Sunrise as we arrive in Los Angeles.

Aviation is a pastime enjoyed by many thousands of people from all over the world and all walks of life. From professional commercial and military pilots, scenic charter and aeromedical pilots, to private aviators who own their own aircraft and fly for recreation. There are many people who decide to fly and the reasons behind why they do so are as wide-ranging as sky they share.

Whether you are interested in aviation and want to learn to fly for recreation or make a career of it, there are many things you must first consider before jumping into an aircraft.

Learning to fly is not only financially demanding and challenging, but it can also be very frustrating when you can't fly due to a plane breaking down or inclement weather requiring rescheduling of your lesson.

In saying that, there is nothing quite like being able to take the controls of an aircraft yourself. The responsibilities, duties and worries that once overwhelmed you seem to fade away as you leave the ground. Flying is an incredibly rewarding career or pastime, with unique challenges that are faced each day. Every pilot that I know is proud to go to work each and every day.

If you are reading this book for the purposes of a career in aviation, obtaining your commercial licence and getting paid to fly an aircraft, life surely can't get any better! As one of the most enviable careers in the world, being a commercial pilot allows you to work in a moving office where every day is different and challenging. Aviation is a rewarding career and most pilots I know are proud and lucky to have a job that others envy.

This book focusses primarily on people who are wanting to learn to fly as a commercial pilot, but there is also a valuable wealth of knowledge for people just wanting to fly for fun and recreation. In a nutshell, this book contains valuable information relating to licensing and medicals, flying schools, gaining your first elusive job, and the airlines.

I wrote this book because when I learnt to fly I didn't know the first thing about aviation. I found that there wasn't a lot of information available to people like myself about what I should do before approaching a flying school, how to pick the right flying school for my needs, and how I would use my new and shiny commercial licence to land my first flying job. The same still holds true today; pilots who are starting out lack the knowledge that others know in regards to the industry, which could help them avoid frustration and save money.

Aviation is a difficult and expensive career path to break into. It is only after you have committed quite a deal of time and money in the aviation industry that you begin to fully understand its nature and pitfalls associated with the industry. With practical hints and tips and written in an easy to read format, I hope this book can help you answer all of your questions regarding the flight training process, career progression and what to do to find that elusive first job. I also sincerely hope that it answers some questions that you may not even have thought of and will give you a valuable insight into the aviation industry, which could in turn potentially save you thousands of dollars, time and painful frustration.

If you train, study and prepare well for a career in aviation, you will find it can carry you a long way to being successful in the aviation industry. Planning a career in the aviation industry is as important as gaining the right qualifications to become a pilot in the first place. As you continue through your aviation journey, you will hear of our industry being compared to a game of snakes and ladders. I have been lucky in that apart from a few setbacks and extended periods of time looking for a suitable job, I have been able to progress through the aviation industry and from job to job without much hassle. Some others have not been so lucky and have found that they have been retrenched by one, two or even three different jobs due to bankruptcy of the company or through redundancies. Perseverance and a mentality of "never give up" will ensure that you make it through the tough times.

Before we start, I would just like to say a big thank you to Matt, Salah, Elle, Etienne, John and Sam for their stories in chapter nine. They have taken the time to remember their aviation journey and how they got to where they are today so that you, as a reader, can gain a better understanding of how pilots start off in the aviation industry and the challenges they face.

I knew from a very young age that I wanted to be a pilot. It comes as no surprise with my Father having worked for *Qantas* for the previous 35 years as a long-haul flight attendant and my Mother previously holding a private pilot's licence, also working at *Qantas* as a flight attendant and currently working with *Virgin Australia* in guest relations and ground staff. Having been very passionate about aviation from visiting the fight deck a number of occasions for takeoff and landing, I was about seven years of age when my interest in aviation sparked and I decided that I wanted to be an airline pilot.

I started my flying in Grade 10 through the Australian Air Force Cadets and studied subjects including physics and math at school. After completing high school I enrolled with a flight training school at Archerfield in Brisbane and completed my Commercial Pilot's Licence and multi-engine instrument rating over the course of 18 months. I self-studied most of the theory exams requires for the Air Transport Pilots Licence over the course of four months.

At the end of my training I sent out 200 personalized letters and resumes to flying organizations around Australia. I received one reply and that was only to be told that they had no jobs available! I then followed up each letter with a phone call a week later to confirm they had received my resume, but again with no offers or prospects. Undeterred by this I moved away from home at the age of 18 to Kununurra in Western Australia with the hope of obtaining my first flying job. I set myself up and worked a bar job for four months sending resumes out to every scenic and charter operator and visiting them in person every few days. On these visits I would speak to the other pilots and help them wash airplanes in the 40 degree heat. My only reward for this work was the hope that I would be seen by the chief pilot and my willingness to work for nothing would transpire into a future job. After four months of living in Kununurra I was finally offered a job, albeit a ground based one as a refueller position for one year with the chance of flying the year after. All my dreams of flying came quickly to a halt with the realization that I may work for an aviation company for a whole year in a rural area and not clock up any flight hours at all. I was thinking to myself that this was not what I had envisioned when I left home to move to the other side of the country. My fear shortly dissipated, as just before accepting this ground based position I was offered a job flying part time with another scenic operator in Kununurra which I accepted.

My first job was tough but it allowed me to gain over 600 hours in eight months. I soon found out that as an employee, being a pilot was only one of my jobs. Every morning at 5am we had to pre-flight the aircraft, order fuel and then drive the bus and minivans around Kununurra picking up passengers, brief them on what they would see during their scenic flight around the *Bungle Bungles* and then drop those passengers off after their flight. It wasn't uncommon to pick up passengers for our next flight at 9am as we were dropping the others off. After returning from our second 2 hour flight for the day we would generally wash aircraft, check in passengers and help with other general duties around the company – basically anything that was required at the time. Come 2pm we would do everything again for our third flight for the day before finally finishing work at 6pm. All to start again the next day with a 4am wakeup, five days a week.

I was very fortunate to find a house to rent with people I had worked with at the bar, however most of the pilots I knew lived at the local backpackers in a six bedroom dorm for the entire season as they were unable to find other accommodation during the competitive dry season and with no previous rental history as they had just moved away from home like myself.

At the end of the year I travelled to Darwin and had a face to face interview with the Chief Pilot at a large charter company. I was offered a job on the spot, initially employed in operations, answering phone calls, providing quotes for charters, checking in passengers and loading aircraft. After a few months I moved back onto the *Cessna* 206 and 210 I had been flying at my previous company, with the opportunity to move onto the larger twins when a position became available. I eventually started flying the *Cessna 402* and 404 later in the year. After gaining over 800 hours of multi-engine experience and during the GFC, progression to turbines was slow so I decided to take just under two years off my career to travel to Canada on a working holiday visa. This had been a dream of mine since leaving high school and I thought that it would be the best time to do so.

After returning from Canada I spent six months trying to find my next flying job. I quickly found out that, although I had 800 hours on twin *Cessna* 404 aircraft and over 2000 hours total flying time, it was harder to obtain a suitable position than it had been to obtain my first job. Through constant contact with an instructor that had been working at the flying school I studied at who was now the Chief Pilot of a charter company in Darwin, I was offered a ground school with the chance of being offered a First Officer position. After four months I was offered a job and started as a First Officer on my first twin turbine. Mainly doing mining charters and scheduled services, I worked as a First Officer for over a year then became a Captain for 5 months before I was offered a job with two airlines. After much debating, I finally decided on the airline which I thought offered a better lifestyle, promotion to

Captain in a shorter time period and allowed me to live back in Brisbane. I have currently been employed for just over three years and enjoy my career immensely.

It has taken just over eight years from when I left flying school without a job to being employed back on the east coast of Australia. It was probably the hardest time of my life with tough decisions and problems to solve every day that required outside the box thinking and an open mind, however I would never change my time in Kununurra or the Territory for anything else in the world as I have met some amazing people who will be friends for life and experiences like none other.

A brief history of aviation in Australia

Much can be written about the significance of aviation in Australia. Since the *Wright brothers* first flight in North Carolina at the end of 1903, it is no surprise that aviation in Australia has played a major part in our country's history due to the remoteness and vast distances of our continent.

The first person to sustain powered flight in Australia was *Colin Defries* in December 1909, taking off and landing from Victoria Park Raceway in Sydney, covering a distance of 105 meters. The first flight to be recognized by the Aerial League of Australia as the first official flight in Australia however was made in 1910 by the great illusionist *Harry Houdini*. He covered a distance of 10 kilometers in the town of Diggers Rest, Victoria which is not that far from where Melbourne International Airport lies today in his Voisin Biplane.

In 1920 *Wilmot Hudson Fysh* and *Paul McGinness* both Australian Flying Corp Officers were surveying an air race route between Longreach and Katherine. Over the flight they were convinced that an air service would be able to link remote outback settlements. With grazier *Fergus McMaster* for financial backing, Queensland Northern Territory Aerial Services was registered in Winton Queensland on the 16th of November 1920. This was the beginning of what we now know as *QANTAS*.

In 1935, the Australian government threatened to legislate private road transport operators in an attempt to stop the demise of Victorian Railways due to private freight and passenger transport operators taking away from its business. *Sir Reg Ansett*, who was a road transport businessman at the time founded his own airline, *Ansett Airways*.

Since then, commercial aviation has changed dramatically, with the technological advancements made during the Second World War, the introduction of the Jet Age in the 1950s, the rise and fall of startup airlines business and the privatization of aviation in Australia.

The aviation industry today

Today, aviation in Australia is still as important as it was during the early days of the Pioneers; not only with commercial flights daily to every capital city, and also most other major towns, but through the network of charter operators servicing the mining industry and remote locations, including aboriginal communities.

With the introduction of low cost carriers, it has also allowed more people to travel more often. The safety of airline travel is also unprecedented, with aviation having gone from little over nothing at the start of the 19th century, to nearly perfected in the 21st century.

In the civil world, CASA - the *Civil Aviation Safety Authority,* is the government body that regulates the aviation industry within Australia. This includes primary responsibility for the rules of the air, policy, licensing and maintenance. Air traffic services and other aviation related services are provided by a private company regulated by CASA called *Air Services Australia* (ASA).

The Australian Transport Safety Bureau (ATSB) works in conjunction with CASA and is a non-judgmental government body that assists to increase safety of aviation in Australia through recommendations and findings of previous accidents and incidents.

Difficulties facing the aviation industry in Australia

All industries go through varying degrees of highs and lows with aviation being no different. Aviation as a whole however is somewhat more susceptible to external factors than other industries and is a very volatile industry, affected by many external factors. In the past we have seen issues such as terrorism, the outbreak of SARs and the global financial crisis have massive effects on both the international and domestic airline industry.

Aviation is dependent on a number of external industries, one of the largest in Australia being mining. With the recent downturn in commodity prices and slowdown of mining in Australia as a whole, this means less FIFO (fly in fly out) operations and flights associated with this industry.

There are also many future problems facing the aviation industry in Australia. One such is an ageing general aviation fleet. With the increase of public liability in America since the 1980's; the main manufacturers of light aircraft that are used for general aviation in Australia have declined to the point where most general aviation aircraft in Australia are over 30 years old. Newer aircraft manufacturers such as Diamond and Cirrus have started to manufacture light twin aircraft for the purpose of flight training and we are seeing more and more schools adopting these modern aircraft. It is a fact however that most general aviation companies throughout Australia still operate aircraft that are 30 years old, including the Cessna 206, 210, Beechcraft Baron, Cessna 404 and Piper chieftain to name a few.

Increasing fuel prices, insurance, litigation and the emerging threat of terrorism are all factors that will shape the Australia airline industry in the years to come.

For airlines, a major difficulty that will be faced in the future is the looming pilot shortage. As discussed in the updated, chapter 1, *Boeing* suggests that an additional 790,000 pilots will be required over the next 20 years. Although a difficulty for employers, now more than ever has it been a great time to be a pilot.

Acronyms used in this book

In aviation, acronyms abound. From AIP, IFR, NDB VOR, to VMC, almost everything can be shorted to an acronym and it can get confusing at times. At the end of this book is a glossary of all terms used in this book.

Who are pilots?

Pilots come for a wide and varied background of cultures, age, race and values. If however you were to ask a group of pilots what the main attributes they considered they either fitted into or thought were more important for a successful career in the aviation industry, they would probably describe the following:

✈ Technically minded as oppose to creative minded

✈ Ability to handle stress under pressure

✈ Good communication skills

✈ Ability to work well as a team and autonomously as required

✈ Future team leader potential (Captain)

✈ Passion for flying and aviation in general

The pros and cons of being a pilot

Before we start on our journey through this book, I thought it would be prudent to start with a quick outline of some of the positive and negative aspects of becoming a pilot. As with any job or career, the good also comes with the bad, and the same holds true for the life of a pilot.

Many pilots get involved in the aviation industry for reasons other than money. Most pilots I know had an innate passion for aviation and flying from a very young age. Maybe their family members were involved in the aviation industry, they were able to visit the cockpit before or after a flight as a passenger, or perhaps they panned their head skywards every time a jet flew overhead in awe.

I'm sure that you can relate to one of the above scenarios. I have written a list of some of the advantages and disadvantages of a career in the aviation industry as a pilot which is detailed on the following page.

Advantages

✈ Work hours

Working as a pilot can have great work hours. Depending on the job and the rostering, as a pilot you may work as little as 10 hours a week. Likewise, in a monthly roster you may find that you have four days off in a row, much more than the normal weekend of any office worker. Because pilots are expected to work public holidays and weekends with no penalties, we are given 6 weeks of annual leave per annum.

✈ High Quality of Living

Later in this book, I detail the expected base salaries of different pilot positions within Australia. Although starting salaries are less than the average Australian wage and even abysmal; after a few years you will be earning a decent salary with the expectation that this will rise as you progress from job to job and from first officer to captain positions.

✈ Sense of pride

Most pilots I know are proud to have a career as a pilot and enjoy their job immensely. There is a wonderful sense of achievement after flying a plane with skill and precision, in passing your next licence or exam or check flight.

✈ Company perks

As an employee you may be entitled to benefits such as discounted flights, hotel and holidays. This is dependent on the company you work for and is usually only available when working for larger airlines.

✈ Unique Office

You will have an office with an amazing view every day. It's a mix of working an inside and outside job at the same time. Sure there may be times when you need to sign on at 4am whilst it is still dark but instead of sitting down to work in an office, you will get to experience the amazing view as the sun rises over the rest of the population. The views are always changing and the working environment is in a constant dynamic.

Disadvantages

✈   Work hours

Although I also categorized this as an advantage, the hours of work as a pilot can also be extremely frustrating or fatiguing. You may have a 4am sign-on with a 10-12 hour shift, 3 or 4 days in a row.

Pilots are also expected to work shift and back of the clock duties, however how many of these shifts you do is also dependent on the company you work for and aircraft type you operate.

Pilots work weekends and public holidays. This might mean that you are working all day Saturday and all Sunday. It may even mean that you work Christmas Eve, Christmas, New Year's Eve and New Year's Day. Aviation never stops, it is a 24/7/365 operation. When your friends or family are at home or out having a good time you may find yourself signing on for an 8 hour duty.

You may also have plans after work but due to weather or aircraft breakdown you find that you are delayed from arriving back home one or even five hours after you thought you might have been. If the plane is broken or the weather is bad enough you may even find yourself stranded for an unscheduled overnight at whichever airport you are at.

✈ Passing medicals and staying fit

Every year a pilot you must pass a medical to ensure that they are safe to operate a plane. The slightest problem may mean that you temporarily lose your licence for a period of months or even permanently.

✈ Pressure

Especially so of your first job, you might be pressured by your boss or the owner to bend the rules to get the job done. Other pressures include weather, breakdowns and making decisions under tough conditions.

✈ Simulator and line checks

Once you start flying larger aircraft and operating under the IFR (instrument flight rules) you will be expected to complete any number of checks including instrument rating renewals, simulator or cyclic checks and line checks. Approximately every six months you are expected to prove yourself to ensure that you are capable of flying a plane in every operating condition and both normal and emergency procedures. If you fail more than once you may find yourself in the unenviable position of searching for another job.

Avenues into aviation

There are many ways that a person can become a pilot. Below is a simple diagram showing the different avenues into aviation. You can either join the military (Navy, Army or Air Force) and get paid to learn how to fly, complete your licences through a civil flying school or be successful in obtaining a cadetship through certain airlines. All three avenues into an aviation career are discussed in this book, with the main focus on civilian flying through a flying school explained in detail later in the book.

The diagram below is an expanded version of the above flowchart.

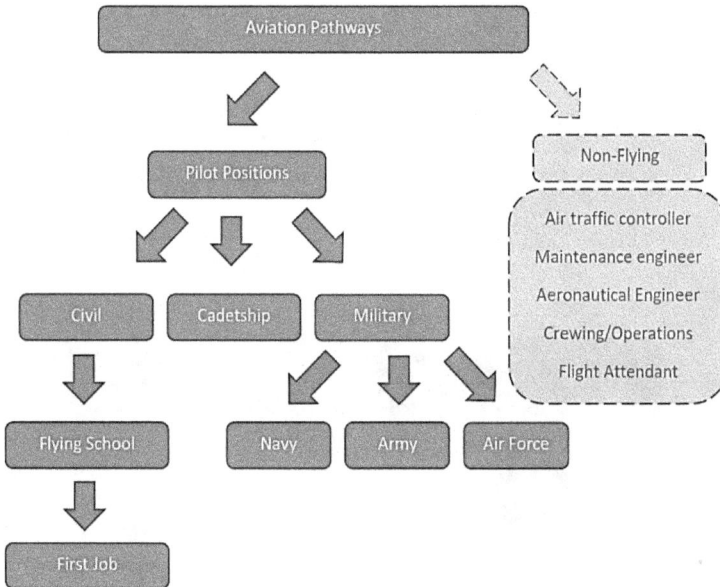

Airforce

Other than learning to fly through a school or airline cadet program, joining the Australian Air Force is another avenue to becoming a pilot.

<u>Eligibility</u>

The following eligibility flowchart will help assess whether you may be able to gain a position as a pilot with the Australian Defence Force.

Australian Citizen

⬇

Over 17 Years Old

(16 for ADFA)

⬇

Completion of year 12

⬇

Passes in English, Math + 2 other subjects

(These eligibility and fitness requirements are subject to change so it would be best to confirm the above information before assessing your suitability)

⬇

Fit + Healthy

(To pass fitness test)

⬇

BMI + Weight

(See right)

⤑

BMI = 18.5 – 29.9

Weight = 55 – 100kg

Height - 163cm to 193cm

Sitting Height - 100cm max

Buttock to knee length - 67cm max

Buttock to heel length - 122cm max

Application Process

At the time of writing, the following process is required to apply to become a pilot with the Australian Defence Force.

The first step in the process is to create an application. This can be done either online or calling the Defence Force recruitment team on 13 19 01.

After applying you should be contacted by a Defence Force recruitment team member who will then be able to book you in for a *YOU Session* which stands for *Your Opportunities Unlimited*.

The *YOU* session will take place at one of the ADF recruitment centers based around the country. The day consists of a quick rundown of the Defence Force followed by an aptitude test conducted on a computer which will then be assessed by a recruitment team member who will print out a *job opportunity* report which is a list of jobs that you have qualified for.

After the YOU session, you will then conduct an interview with a Defence careers counsellor to assess your eligibility and suitability for the Defence Force. This includes which positions within the Defence Force you would be most suited in, causing answering a number of other questions relating to your application such as motivation and attitude, enthusiasm, roles, training, general life in the Defence Force and rights and responsibilities.

You will also be required to submit supporting documentation such as educational passes, birth certificate and drivers licence. A police check will also be conducted.

After this you will need to complete an assessment day. An over the phone interview will be conducted with a recruiter prior to the assessment day that will help you prepare for the interview and what you need to know.

The assessment day should be treated as an interview like any other type of job or career you would be apply for. It will consists of an interview and medical.

Training

If successful with your application you can decide whether you would also like to complete a degree through the *Australian Defence Force Academy* (ADFA) as well as pilot training. Completing a degree however is not mandatory.

```
┌─────────────────────────┐
│  Successful Application  │
└─────────────────────────┘
        ↙           ↘
┌──────────────────┐   ┌──────────────────┐
│  ADFA Training   │   │ Officer Training │
│                  │   │                  │
│ (includes Officer│   │                  │
│    Training)     │   │                  │
└──────────────────┘   └──────────────────┘
                              │
                              ↓
                  ┌──────────────────┐
                  │ Pilot Basic      │
                  │ Training         │
                  │ (Phase 1)        │
                  └──────────────────┘
                              │
                              ↓
                  ┌──────────────────┐
                  │ Pilot Basic      │
                  │ Training         │
                  │ (Phase 2)        │
                  └──────────────────┘
```

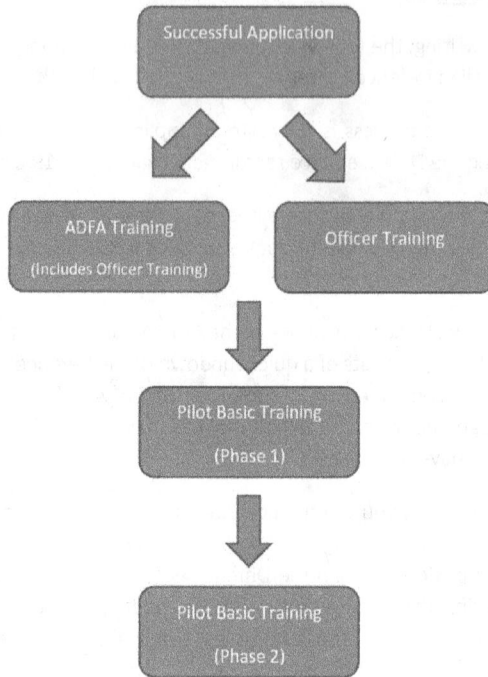

Officer Training

Officer training is conducted over 17 weeks. If studying a degree through ADFA an additional 6 hours per week is included as part of the ADFA training that includes officer training plus an additional 6 weeks.

Pilot Basic Training

Pilot training is completed over the course of just over 6 months in a single engine piston training aircraft called the *CT4B Airtrainer*.

The training is conducted over 2 phases that include the following sequences:

PHASE 1

✈ General introduction to flying including emergency procedures and stalls, spins and aerobatic flying

✈ Night and instrument flying

✈ Navigation

PHASE 2

Ground training and briefing including topics such as aerodynamics, systems, meteorology, airmanship, situational awareness and ATC.

✈ Continued focus on flying skills

✈ More advanced aerobatics

✈ Emergency procedures

Pilot Advanced Training

Once basic training is completed, you will then move onto the *Pilatus PC21*. The PC12 is a sophisticated single engine turbine training aircraft that can be used for initial jet training at a fraction of the cost of training jets. Advanced pilot training is conducted over the course of approximately 9 months. Training includes:

✈ Consolidating already learned sequences and skills on a higher performance aircraft

✈ Low level navigation

✈ Formation flying

Aircraft Placement

After basic and advanced training, depending on proficiency, ability and the requirements of the Defence Force at the specific time, you will be placed onto a certain aircraft or fleet including military fighter jets, or large turboprop aircraft.

Women's Graduate Pilot Scheme

Among other universities, *Griffith University* offers students a course called the *Bachelor of Aviation*. If you are a female, already studying this course offered through *Griffith* you may be eligible to apply for the Defence Force through the *Graduate Pilot Scheme* (GPS). More details can be found on the Australian Defence Force recruitment page or contacting a recruiter via phone.

Period of service

Applying for a position as a pilot with the Australian Defence Force means that you will be paid to complete your pilot training. For this reason, the Defence Force has a minimum period of service called the *Initial Minimum Period of Service (IMPS)*. At the time of writing this was for a minimum time of 11.5 years, with candidates who elect to study a degree through ADFA for a minimum period of 14.5 years.

Candidates that apply through the GPS described above however may be subject to a reduced period of service as little as 3 years.

Benefits of learning to fly through the Defence Force

Some medical restrictions and other eligibility criteria such as those outlined in the flowchart previously discussed exclude some people from learning to fly through the Defence Force however for the most part, there are many benefits to learning to fly through the Defence Force.

To become a fully fledged pilot through the Australian Defence Force, it will cost you no money of your own and you will actually be paid whilst you train. Accommodation and meals will also be provided. The expected salary of a pilot once they have completed between 1.5 -2 years of training is approximately $80,000 to $90,000 per annum.

Benefits of a career with the Defence Force can be researched on the Australian Defence Force website however some include free medical and dental cover and rental assistance.

Cadetship

Many airlines with either jet or turboprop aircraft offer people with little or no prior flying experience what is called a *Cadetship*. This usually means that the airline will pay for that person's initial training and then offer them a position within the company as either a first or second officer, depending on the program. Cadetships are a great way to enter the aviation industry as some airlines will start paying your salary during flying training. For a detailed discussion of the specific cadetships, see the first chapter, update for 2019. Below is a brief summary of cadetships.

Cadetship Minimum requirements

Cadetships are offered through many different regional and airline employers. The minimum requirements to be able to apply for a cadetship vary depending on the position that you are applying for.

Bonding

Depending on the type of cadet program, you may be required to pay for the course itself, it may be deducted from your salary once employed or your employer may pay for your training costs. Obviously if an airline is going to invest a lot of time and money into a single person, in return they expect them to stay with the company for a certain period of time. Like the minimum period of service through the Defence Force, cadet programs usually ask for a certain amount of time after training that the pilot will serve the company as an employee. This is normally called a bonding period. The bonding period differs from airline to airline however can run up to seven years of service. If you leave before the period of expected service you may be liable to pay a certain amount of money for leaving your contract early.

Benefits of learning to fly through a cadet program

Cadet programs can offer people an outstanding career opportunity. It allows some candidates the ability to learn to become a pilot for those that would otherwise not be in a financial position to learn through a flying school. Cadet programs can also fast track your career in that you may be flying as a first officer on a multi crew turboprop or jet in as little as 12 months.

With the benefits of cadet programs also comes a few matters that any person seriously looking at a cadet program should consider. In the unlikely event that the company you are training with becomes bankrupt or closes down for any reason or you fail your training, you may be liable to pay for any training costs incurred by the company. It is best to check the individual company and ask so that you have a thorough understanding of their conditions and all possible outcomes.

Who can learn how to fly?

Just about anyone can learn to fly, however there are a few medical and age restrictions. You may start flying training as young as you want, however you cannot complete your first solo until the age of 15. You may not hold a Private Pilots Licence until the age of 17, a Commercial Pilots Licence (CPL) until you turn 18 or an Air Transport Pilots Licence (ATPL) until 21. Likewise there are some medical restrictions such as epilepsy and diabetes that unfortunately stop some people from being able to fly.

What type of pre educational requirements are required to start flying?

The requirements to start flying training with a civilian school vary from school to school. Some require students to have undertaken and completed year 12 whilst others do not have any high school requirements but do recommend that a good understanding of Physic, Math and English as these are the main subjects that aviation and flying are based around.

Most airlines require these subjects to be passed to at least a year 10 level and some cadetships require high passes in Physics, Math and English at a grade 12 level. Studying subjects that are related to aviation such as Physics, Math and English at school is recommended and highly valuable as you may find that some subjects and topics covered in higher level theory examinations such as those in the Commercial Pilots Licence and Air Transport Pilots Licence contain information relating to the above subjects.

Preparing for flying training during school

A good understanding of aviation comes from a well-rounded knowledge of the principles that effect an aircraft and the decision making process of a pilot on a day to day level. Communication starts in the crew room between the Captain and the Co-Pilot but also extends to the rest of the crew, operations, rostering, your Chief Pilot, the refueller and even the ground handlers who load the plane.

Flight planning and refueling involve a lot of numbers, calculations and rules of thumb. In the air, pilots are constantly updating figures and checking navigation. Throughout this, we are flying an aircraft that can weigh several hundred tonne, through weather that is constantly changing and evolving. To this end, from this brief paragraph above, you can see that a thorough understand of english, physics and math is an important basis to a good understanding of aviation.

My recommendation would be to study at least these three subjects in high school. Other subjects that can benefit becoming a pilot, but are not necessarily as important nor required are chemistry and geography.

Trial Introductory Flight

The first flight that a person can conduct is what is called a *Trial Introductory Flight* or TIF. A TIF is a 20-45 minute flight with an instructor that allows you to feel what it's like to fly and take the controls of an aircraft. It is also especially perfect if you are unsure whether flying is your cup of tea. Depending on the flying school, a TIF usually starts with a briefing about basic aviation concepts and what you can expect from the flight. The flight instructor will then show you around the aircraft in what is called a pre-flight to check that everything is in working order before takeoff. Once airborne, you will go through a few normal maneuvers including climbing, descending, turning, and perhaps even touch and go landings, all in a flight that lasts between 20-45 minutes. After the flight you will have a debriefing and you will be able to ask your instructor any questions you may have relating to aviation or starting flying training.

A TIF is an optional flight that is it is not required for the licensing syllabus. If you are certain you want to become a pilot you can skip this flight and start your flying lessons with a flying school.

ARN

The first step in flight training should be to obtain an *Aviation Reference Number* (ARN) from CASA. It is a unique number not only given to pilots, but also other professionals within the aviation industry such as air traffic controllers. It is quoted each time you speak with CASA or fill out paperwork. Applying for an ARN is free and it must be obtained before you can conduct your medical examination. More information about ARNs may be obtained on the CASA website www.casa.gov.au

(form 1162 if you search CASAs online form register by number). ARNs are an electronic number much like your tax file number.

Medical

The next step in the process is obtaining an aviation medical. Before you are able to conduct your first solo flight you must first pass a Medical Examination by a CASA approved medical examiner called a *Designated Aviation Medical Examiner* (DAME). They will then issue you with a medical certificate. Make sure that you have a medical conducted by a DAME and not your local GP. Some people have called their GP explaining they need a medical before starting their flying training, to be told that they can be conducted. When they submit this "medical" to CASA, only then do they find out that it is not recognized, after spending a lot of time, money and effort only to start to process over again.

A complete list of CASA approved DAMEs can be found on the CASA website.

There are three types of medical certificates available to pilots depending on what type of flying being conducted and what type of licence they intend to hold.

CLASS 1

This medical applies to holders of Air Transport Pilot Licences (ATPL) and Commercial Pilot Licences (CPL). Basically those that use their licence for monetary reasons or have a job as a pilot.

CLASS 2

This medical applies to holders of Recreational Pilots Licences (RPL), and Private Pilots Licences (PPL). This is the minimum medical required for people starting their flying training or for those that fly for the purposes of recreation. A cass 2 medical can now be held by an instructor.

RAMPC

In 2014 new government regulations came into effect called Part 61 which means that those people wishing to obtain a Recreational Pilots Licence may instead of getting a Class 2 medical obtain a RAMPC which stands for *Recreational Medical practitioner's Certificate*.

If you want to learn to fly for the purpose of gaining a career in the aviation industry it is strongly recommend that you obtain a Class 1 medical rather than a Class 2 and that you do so before you start flying training. This is the most restrictive and thorough medical examination and will be required when you start a career as a pilot anyway.

The Class 1 medical will find any medical problems or discrepancies that may otherwise prevent you from being able to hold an unrestricted medical certificate that may not be found with the less thorough Class 2 medical. It is better to pay the extra fee to obtain the class 1 medical upfront than to have spent thousands of dollars and perhaps years training to be a pilot only to find out later that a medical restriction prevents you from being a commercial pilot.

The validity period of a medical depends on its class. A Class 1 medical is valid for 12 months (that is you must renew it each year), whereas a Class 2 or RAMPC medical is less restrictive and lasts four years. A medical must be conducted before the expiry date and if passed, the DAME will stamp the old medical to extend its validity for an extra four months whilst CASA processes the new one. Unfortunately the aviation medical cannot be bulk billed through Medicare.

What to expect in the medical and how much will it cost

The costs of obtaining a medical depends on if it's your initial or recurrent medical, and also on specific age-related testing.

For an initial medical there are many different parts including a consultation with a DAME, ophthalmological examination and blood test. Medical renewals each year after that only require a consultation with a DAME with special tests required when the medical is completed at certain ages (see next chapter for a list of tests).

The DAME consultation is the first step and this includes a urine sample, approximately 50 yes or no health related questions, general checkup, hearing test, basic eye test and ECG test. Depending on the DAME this test can cost between $200-300 and is not bulk billable or claimable on private health insurance.

Make sure that you drink enough liquid before your medical. For the urine test you must be able to fill the jar to a certain point but at the same time but not too much that your urine is diluted to the point where it can't be tested. Either one will mean you might have to come back to re-sit that part of the test.

It is also recommended that prior to the hearing test you don't listen to any very loud music or noise so that you give your ears the best chance to hear all the frequencies during the sensitive test.

Having poor eyesight is generally not a problem for holding a medical, as long as it can be improved by vision correction such as glasses or contact lenses. At the time of writing, the rules and regulations surrounding the medical implications of color blindness were changing. It would be best to contact CASA or a DAME in regards to color blindness and its effects on owning a licence.

After the medical you will need to book a consultation with an ophthalmologist who will conduct specific eye related tests. You can either ask for a recommendation from the DAME or book this at the same time as the medical so you don't have to wait another two weeks for the next part of the medical process. The ophthalmologist exam can cost between $200-300.

For the eye test make sure you bring any correction vision should you wear any and if you use contact lenses, a contact lens case with fluid as you will need to remove them for the test. It is not advisable to drive immediately after the eye test as the ophthalmologist will place a chemical eye drop in your eye that tests for scarring and cataracts.

The next step is blood testing at an approved medical testing center. This costs approximately $100.

After you have finished your medical examination, the DAME will submit your results to CASA. There is a $75 fee payable directly to CASA online for the processing of the medical application. Make sure that you fill this form out correctly and that your DAME submits it with the medical paperwork as you might find out a few weeks later that your medical hasn't been processed. All in all, your first medical may cost you around $500 to $700. The CASA website states that medicals can take up to 28 days to process so make sure you book a DAME and ophthalmologist in advance early

Age related testing

Depending on your age when you complete or renew your medical is what will determine which type of "age specific" testing that may be required above and beyond a normal medial certificate. Below is a table which outlines the different reports and tests that may need to be carried out for a Class 1 medical. Note that Class 2 medicals do not require the below additional tests to be carried out unless otherwise clinically indicated.

AGE	SER. LIP. BI. GI*	AUDIO	EYE	ECG	CVD RISK SCORE
INITIAL ISSUE					
ALL	•	•	•	•	•
RENEWAL					
25	•	•		•	•
30	•	•		•	•
32				•	
34				•	
35	•	•			•
36				•	
38				•	
40	•	•		•	•
45	•	•		•	•
50	•	•		•	•
55	•	•		•	•

* SER. LIP. BI. GI refers to fasting serum lipids test and fasting blood glucose test

Licences

As of the 1st September 2014, the rules regarding pilot licences changed to more closely align Australian regulations with other countries throughout the world. Previously you would have had to apply for Student Pilots licence (SPL) before going solo. Now, all you need is a medical and ARN. The following is a list of all the licences a pilot in Australia can hold and the order in which they are obtained:

✈ RPL Recreational Pilot Licence (RPL)

> Allows a pilot to fly in the training area

✈ PPL Private Pilots Licence (PPL)

> Allows a pilot to fly anywhere within Australia with non-paying or cost sharing passengers

✈ CPL Commercial Pilots Licence (CPL)

> Allows a pilot to fly anywhere within Australia with passengers and charge for their service

✈ ATPL Air Transport Pilot Licence (ATPL)

> Allows a pilot to be a Captain of a multi-crew aircraft

Most people believe that obtaining a commercial pilots licence allows them to fly large jet aircraft. This is not the case. A CPL allows a pilot to fly any type of aircraft as pilot in command for monetary value (scenic, charter or instructing). An ATPL only adds the additional privilege of being able to fly a multi crew aircraft as a Captain. Once a licence is obtained it is perpetual meaning that it never expires.

In between the licences there are qualifications and ratings that a pilot can obtain that allows them to fly different aircraft with features and in certain conditions. For example a *Night VFR Rating* (NVFR) allows a pilot to fly at night. A complete list of all the licences and qualifications that a pilot may wish to obtain are set out in an easy to read flow chart later in the book.

Aviation Security Identification Card

In addition to all of the above, some airports also require you to obtain an *Aviation Security Identification Card* (ASIC). There airports are called *security controlled aerodromes*. Security controlled aerodromes are normally those that have regular scheduled services operating out of them. Most of these airports have an area which is security controlled however the remainder of the airport is not security controlled and an ASIC is not required in those areas (which include the flying schools). You should check whether you will need a ASIC by contacting your flying school, the airport or Department of Infrastructure and regional development (DOTARS) at 02 6274 7111 or publicaffairs@infrastructure.gov.au. The cost of an ASIC is $200.5 ($98.50 if under 18 years of age) and takes approximately four weeks to process.

Obtaining everything in the correct order

Your first step in your aviation journey should be to apply for an ARN. You must have an ARN before your medical and a medical before your first solo (usually occurring after you have gained between 10-20 flight hours). An ASIC may also be required if you fly at a security controlled aerodrome.

If you complete the licences and medicals in the order outlined below you can avoid lengthy delays while waiting for an ARN to do a medical or a medical to fly solo.

```
┌──────────────┐
│     TIF      │
│  (Optional)  │
└──────────────┘
        │
        ▼
┌──────────────┐
│     ARN      │
│(Before Medical)│
└──────────────┘
        │
        ▼
┌──────────────┐        ┌ ─ ─ ─ ─ ─ ─ ─ ─ ─ ┐
│   Medical    │          Includes DAME medical,
│              │          ophthalmologist and
│(Before first solo)│      blood test
└──────────────┘        └ ─ ─ ─ ─ ─ ─ ─ ─ ─ ┘
        │
        ▼
┌ ─ ─ ─ ─ ─ ─ ┐
│     ASIC     │
│ (if required)│
└ ─ ─ ─ ─ ─ ─ ┘
        │
        ▼
┌──────────────┐
│ Flying Lessons │
│(Including first solo)│
└──────────────┘
```

Should you obtain a university degree?

You do not require any formal qualifications or university degrees to become a pilot, however there are many universities offering aviation courses and degrees that allow students to complete an aviation degree.

Most general aviation operators and those that employ first time pilots don't look at university degrees, but hours, competency and other skills they might be able to utilise, including computer literacy and personality and disposition. These skills and qualities are more beneficial to the employer because it allows them to use you during the downtime that you may not be flying.

In saying that, once you start applying for positions in an airline, most will look favourably on a university degree. however this doesn't have to be an aviation related degree, as any degree will show your future employer that you are capable of studying and applying yourself. Skills and expertise in areas such as IT, Economics, and Business Management can make you more employable because you could take up a managerial or desk role later in your career with that airline.

Doing a degree outside of aviation also allows you to fall back on a career external to aviation should you feel you want to change career at a later date, move into a managerial position within an airline, or seek change due to loss of licence or medical.

On the flip-side of the coin, aviation specific degrees cover a wide range of aviation subjects, including Airline Management, Crew Resource Management (CRM), Economics and Engineering. This can be advantageous as a general knowledge of the aviation industry. Airlines look positively upon such well-rounded individuals and it makes sense to have a wider understanding of the industry you intend to be a part of. In saying that, all topics specifically related to a pilot's job are covered in the theoretical exams undertaken to gain a Commercial Pilots Licence.

Depending on how the course is structured, it is worth noting that by doing an aviation related degree and studying to become a pilot, you may have both a University and flying training debt which could run to anywhere between approximately $80,000 to $120,000. Before enrolling for a university degree you should make sure to ask whether the course includes the flying training component.

Every university is different in how they operate - for example, with *Griffith University* the *Bachelor of Aviation* can be taken concurrently with the *Graduate Diploma of Flight Management* program. The *Bachelor of Aviation* includes all of the theoretical components of the course whilst the Diploma includes all of the flight components. With the *University of Southern Queensland*, however if you study the *Bachelor of Aviation (Flight Operations)* you will begin to learn the theoretical components of flight during your first year of university and then during second year begin flying training with a flying school registered with the university. The time and cost involved with the flying aspect however is outside and above what is required of the university degree itself.

Some universities offer scholarships which could significantly decrease the cost of a degree. At the time of writing, the following universities offered aviation courses and degrees tailored towards pilots (universities offer many type of aviation degrees including management, maintenance and many more).

UNIVERSITY	COURSE	LOCATION
University of NSW	Bachelor Aviation – Flying Stream	Bankstown, NSW
University of NSW	Graduate Diploma in Flying	Bankstown, NSW
Griffith University	Bachelor of Aviation	Nathan, QLD
Griffith University	Graduate Diploma of Flight Management	Nathan/Archerfield QLD
RMIT University	Associate Degree in Aviation	Point Cook, VIC
University of South Australia	Bachelor of Aviation	Mawson Lakes, SA
Edith Cowan University	Bachelor of Aviation	Joondalup, WA
University of Southern Queensland	Bachelor of Aviation	Springfield, QLD
Swinburne University of Technology	Bachelor of Aviation	Hawthorne, VIC

What should you look for when researching flying schools?

While each may have the ability to train you for the licence or rating you seek, flying school are different in many ways. The aircraft, instructor experience, syllabus design and delivery methods between different schools can be considerably different from school to school. When looking for a flying school or aero club to start flying training, you want be assured that you are getting the maximum amount of quality and value from your money. Do not look for the cheapest deal or the school that guarantees being able to complete your training in X amount of dollars. What happens if you need extra training or fail to complete a flight test?

You must also choose a flying school based on your current goals and what you would like to achieve as an end result. If you have decided you want to fly as a career and want to complete your commercial pilots licence there may be little point in starting flying training with a school that does not offer that. Some recreational flying schools only offer flying training up to a private pilots licence level.

Like buying a house or unit, look at as many flying schools and aero clubs as you possibly can to gain a good understanding of the differences between each, and what you believe will suit your own needs the best.

Instructors

Most flying schools will have a variety of instructors, and ideally you will want to look for such schools. Flight instructors are able to obtain three different grades or levels - these are 1, 2 and 3 - with 1 being the highest. As becoming an instructor is one way that pilots can gain experience during their flying careers, you may find that some grade three instructors might not have much aeronautical experience. This is not a problem, however more important is the attitude of your instructor. Be wary of instructors that are only interested in gaining hours with no passion for training. Instructors that progress through to level 2 and 1 level ratings are normally genuinely interested in teaching others how to fly, and have made a career in deciding to become an instructor.

Planes

In that there are different type of instructors, there are obviously different types of planes that you are able to learn to fly. Most flying schools use aircraft manufactured by Cessna and Piper such as the Cessna 172, 152 , Piper Tomahawk and Piper Cherokee. More and more flying schools however are adopting modern aircraft, including those with glass cockpits such as the Cirrus SR22 and Diamond DA40.

There are advantages and disadvantages to learning to fly in different aircraft but it basically comes down to what aircraft the flying school owns.

Aircraft with glass cockpits makes the information displayed to the pilot more intuitive and easy to read, however if you do decide to go down the charter route once you finish flying training, the aircraft you will be flying during your first job will most likely not be glass cockpit, and there will therefore be an additional learning curve which would not be involved if you were to learn to fly in an older aircraft with the same instrumentation. In saying that, newer aircraft tend to be more reliable with less downtime.

If you are looking at trying to gain employment at a particular company after flying school, where the aircraft flown is the same one as at a particular flying school, it would be wise to learn on that type of aircraft, as you will be more employable.

A detailed list of questions to ask potential flying schools is displayed on the following pages so that you can make the most informed decision as to which flying school to choose for your flying training needs.

Questions to ask potential flying schools

1) How long has your flying school been in operation?

Ideally you will want to learn from a flying school that has been established for a period of time. Flying schools that have been operating for a longer period of time have many advantages. These can include proven and refined syllabuses, dedicated instructors that have been with the company for a number of years, competitive rates, and in house aircraft maintenance.

2) How many instructors do you have?

The school should have a number of instructors so if your trainer goes away on holidays or is sick you can continue your training during this time.

3) What grades are your instructors?

Ideally the school will have different instructors of differing grades including those that are grade one.

4) Will I be taught by one instructor or many?

You should look for a school where you have the opportunity to be instructed by between 2-3 pilots. As much as there is a standard syllabus to follow, being with only one instructor means that you would potentially get only one person's view and their experiences. Having between 2-3 instructors means that you can ask different questions and gain different insights and opinions. Having more than 3 instructors however can be confusing with too many points of view and differing opinions.

If for some reason you don't get on with your instructor, you should ask your course manager or the Chief Pilot for a new instructor that better suits your needs or personality. After all, you are spending a lot of time and money to be able to complete your licence.

5) Do I need to pay upfront any amount of money or installments?

Advantages to paying upfront may mean that you might get a discount overall, however if you decide that flying is not for you, the school shuts down or you lose your medical, you may not be able to recover the money that you have already paid.

Most schools will have a syllabus of the type of aircraft, amount of hours and briefings required for certain licences. This will include a price of how much you may expect to pay. Be careful as the syllabuses shown on flying school websites will normally show the minimum amount of hours required to gain the appropriate licence and you may need additional training or lessons on certain topics. These will usually be charged at the applicable rate offered by the flying school.

6) If the flying school operates charters, is priority given to them?

Some flying schools will also operate and conduct charter work as well as teaching students. When the flying school is not busy with instructing, this means that they continue making profit by utilizing the aircraft for charter work. The downside is that some schools will give preference to charter flights over instructing so it would be worth asking if your flight may get cancelled if a charter flight was to arise.

7) What type of aircraft do you own and how many?

You need to ask what type of aircraft they own and how many. If they only have one of each aircraft this may mean that you need to book your flying lessons weeks in advance before they are booked out by another student. It can also mean that if the aircraft requires maintenance, it will be unavailable. It is best to choose a school that has a variety of aircraft including those that are larger and more advanced, so that when you progress through your training you can move through the fleet onto an aircraft that suits your ability.

For example you might start your training on a *Diamond DA-20* which is a 2 seat trainer (similar to the older *Cessna 152* which flying schools are phasing out), moving onto the *Diamond DA-40* which is a four seat single engine trainer (similar to the *Cessna 172*) after you have completed your GFPT. After flying those single engine aircraft, should you wish to complete your multi engine instrument rating you will then need to move onto a twin engine aircraft. Again, flying schools are phasing out the *Beechcraft Duchess* and other similar twin engine trainers for aircraft such as the *Diamond DA-42* and *Diamond DA-62* aircraft.

8) What type of syllabus do you follow for the training?

Flying schools can either offer an integrated or non-integrated training course. You ideally want to choose a flying school that has a syllabus of training laid out that students follow to complete the licence. An integrated course is a rigorous method of flight training that is designed to ensure that the practical flight training is integrated with ground based theory. Both the flying and theory must be conducted by the same flying school.

An integrated course means that training for a CPL may be completed in as little as 150 hours flying time. This is a reduction of 50 hours flying time from the standard 200 for a non-integrated course. For this reason it is recommended to do an integrated course as it can cut down the amount of flying training for a private licence by five hours and a commercial by fifty and thus the cost and time involved.

The training for a CPL is aimed at achieving a very high standard of flying skill, airmanship and discipline - 150 hours is the absolute minimum amount of hours required by CASA for a CPL. Some flying schools although offering integrated courses may have syllabuses which run to 160 or 180 hours and some students will require additional lessons on top of the 150 hours minimum. A minimum of 150 hours may not get you a job when another pilot who has not completed an integrated course has 200 hours. (I can say with certainty that eventually when you make it to an airline, you will be counting your hours in lots of 'thousands', however for the sake of your fist job, 50 hours may mean the difference between getting the job or not.

Sometimes obtaining your licence at the absolute minimum of 150 hours this may not be possible, for example if you were learning to flying part time or in a location which doesn't not have a flying school able to offer integrated courses.

9) What type of airspace class does this airport operate in?

The air that planes fly in is divided or classified into different types depending on location and height. For example, because airports are normally quite busy with planes taking off and leaving with aircraft arriving for landing from different directions, a type of "airspace" is set up around that airport, normally cylindrical in shape, extending a certain distance from the airport up to a certain height. Depending on how busy that airport is then determines what "classification" of airspace it is, either Class C, D or G (Classes A, B, C, D, E, and G airspace exist but only the three mentioned before are centered around aerodromes).

Some airports are controlled and planes are directed by air traffic controllers whilst at other airports, pilots communicate over the radio and are their own controllers.

It would be prudent to ask the flying school you are looking whether the airport is air traffic controlled or non-controlled airport. If you fly out of a non-controlled you will learn through your training how to operate into a controlled airport and vice versa.

Non-controlled airports can be cheaper to learn at as the landing a service fees may be cheaper.

10) Does your flying school provide VET-FEE HELP?

Some flying schools are approved by the Australian Government *Department of Education and Training* (DET) to offer VET FEE-HELP to students. This means that students can have part or all of their tuition fees paid for by the Australian Government in the form of a loan (like a university degree). More information about paying for flying training is explained later in this chapter.

Differences between a flying school and aero club

Most aero clubs in Australia provide flight training. Aero clubs are non-for profit organisations which cater for the needs of private pilots who are interested in aviation. If you decide to start flight training at an aero club you will have to join as a member of that club. There is a nominal fee that may be paid on joining and also an annual few, although you should check with the aero club you are enquiring about in regards to their fee structure.

By being a member you will usually have access to a wide variety of benefits and events that are outside the flying training yourself. You may also have the opportunity to meet pilots who flying through the aero club and have already competed their flying training.

Events that an aeroclub may organise are flyways, day trips, BBQs and flying competitions. Some flying schools also provide for some of the above events as well and both usually have an annual pilot award night where all staff, instructors and members get together to celebrate the year over dinner.

Flying School locations

The table on the following page shows aerodromes throughout Australia that have flying school based at them. As flying schools open and close regularly, this list is only provided as a guide.

AERODROME	LOCATION	NUMBER OF SCHOOLS	TYPE OF AIRSPACE
ALBANY	WA	1	CLASS G
ALBURY	NSW	2	CLASS D
ALICE SPRINGS	NT	1	CLASS D
ARCHERFIELD	QLD	5	CLASS D
BACCHUS MARSH	VIC	1	CLASS G
BALLARAT	VIC	2	CLASS G
BALLINA	NSW	1	CLASS G
BANKSTOWN	NSW	6	CLASS D
BATHURST	NSW	2	CLASS G
BUNBURY	WA	1	CLASS G
CABOOLTURE	QLD	2	CLASS G
CAIRNS	QLD	2	CLASS C
CALOUNDRA	QLD	2	CLASS G
CAMDEN	NSW	5	CLASS G
CANBERRA	ACT	3	CLASS C
CESSNOCK	NSW	2	CLASS G
COFFS HARBOUR	NSW	2	CLASS G
DARWIN	NT	1	CLASS C
DUBBO	NSW	3	CLASS G
GERALDTON	WA	2	CLASS G
GOLD COAST	QLD	4	CLASS C
ECHUCA	VIC	1	CLASS G
ESSENDON	VIC	3	CLASS C
GOULBURN	NSW	2	CLASS G

GYMPIE	QLD	1	CLASS G
HOBART	TAS	3	CLASS C
HORSHAM	VIC	2	CLASS G
JANDAKOT	WA	7	CLASS D
LAUNCESTON	TAS	1	CLASS D
LISMORE	NSW	1	CLASS G
MACKAY	QLD	2	CLASS D
MAITLAND	NSW	1	CLASS G
MAREEBA	QLD	1	CLASS G
MERIMBULA	NSW	1	CLASS G
MILDURA	VIC	1	CLASS G
MOORABBIN	VIC	9	CLASS D
MOUNT GAMBIER	VIC	1	CLASS G
ORANGE	NSW	2	CLASS G
PARAFIELD	SA	5	CLASS D
PERTH	WA	2	CLASS C
PORT AUGUSTA	SA	1	CLASS G
REDCLIFFE	QLD	2	CLASS G
SALE	VIC	1	CLASS E
SCONE	NSW	2	CLASS G
SHEPPARTON	VIC	2	CLASS G
SUNSHINE COAST	QLD	3	CLASS D
PORT MACQUARIE	NSW	1	CLASS G
TAMWORTH	NSW	3 (VIRGIN)	CLASS G
TOORADIN	VIC	1	CLASS G
TOOWOOMBA	QLD	3	CLASS G
TOOWOOMBA (WEST WELLCAMP)	QLD	1 (QANTAS)	CLASS G
TOWNSVILLE	QLD	3	CLASS D
WAGGA WAGGA	NSW	2	CLASS G
WARRNAMBOOL	NSW	1	CLASS G

How to pay for flying training

Pilot Licences don't come cheap. Even a recreation pilots licence can cost anywhere from $12,000 to $20,000, with a commercial licence costing from $70,000 upwards of $100,000.

Some students who are conducting their training may find that they will work as many hours as they can leading up to training and out this towards their flying, whereas others may work part time whilst flying at the same time. Some people are also able to borrow money from their parents and then pay them back over time once they are employed as a full time pilot. Another option is that it may also be possible to take out a bank loan to pay for flying training however interest with such loans can be quite high.

Some flying schools are approved by the Australian Government Department of Education and Training (DET) and are able to offer VET student loans. This means that students can have part or all of their tuition fees paid for by the Australian Government. For more information regarding the new scheme, please visit the following link:

hwww.education.gov.au/vet-student-loans

Things to note with VET assistance is that you will be required to pay back the money you have borrowed plus interest once you start earning more than a certain amount per annum. Unfortunately, as pilots travel often through the early parts of their careers, they tend to start a family and buy a house later in life, perhaps around the same time that they are expected to pay back their loan. Although it is an abstract though as it may be many, many years away, it is something to consider.

Training on a budget

Many people who want to become pilots either don't have the money nor the resources to be able to apply for a loan for the amount required to obtain all the licences and rating required to be employable. As stated previously, VET FEE-HELP is available through a number of schools however there are other options to be able to fund your flying training including scholarships and *Austudy*.

Cadetships

As stated before, cadetships are a great way to get started in the aviation industry with little or no money.

Scholarships

Some organisations in Australia offer scholarships to aspiring pilots to inspire aviation within Australia. If you are successful with your scholarship application, you may receive an amount of money that you may put towards your flying training costs. Organizations, flying schools and universities that offer scholarships varies from year to year and a quick internet search will show which scholarships you might be eligible to apply for.

Austudy

Financial help is available to full time students through the Australian Government. If you are single you maybe be eligible to apply for up to $433 per fortnight. Full eligibility criteria for Austudy is available at the following website: www.humanservices.gov.au/customer/services/centrelink/austudy

How flying school charge for lessons

As flying school charge for lessons and licences in different ways this section will focus on what to look for when deciding on a flying school to ensure you not only understand how they charge but also to ensure you receive a competitive rate for your training needs.

Pay as you go/per hour

Some flying schools may offer the method of paying per each flying lesson or hour as you go. The advantages to this are that if you decide for any reason to cancel your training you will not forfeit any prepaid fees.

Prepaid

Some schools may also ask for a certain amount of money to be paid upfront such as a course establishment fee to secure a spot on a PPL or CPL course. Most flying schools will also ask for a certain amount of money to be paid up front, for example $5000. When you have completed flying training up to the amount of approximately $5000, you will then need to "top up" your account with more money to continue training.

Upfront

Some flying schools may also ask to pay for the expected price of the course and then any additional flying training is charged at the applicable rate. For example, if a flying school is advertising a CPL course for $30,000 you would pay this money up front and if you needed any extra flying hours or briefings over the minimum required these would be charged on top of the $30,000.

VET

Some flying schools offer VET fee help, whereby you complete your training though a particular approved course and you would start to repay your loan once you earn above the minimum threshold (at the time of writing approximately $52,000 pa gross).

Checking Bills

Regardless of how you are charged for your lessons, make sure that you look over your statements and invoices carefully for errors. Normally, flying hours flown will be typed into the computer manually by a staff member from the aircraft logbook. Inevitably as human errors do occur, any typing error may result in being overcharged for lessons. For this reason, it would be a good idea to keep a small notepad where you can write down the date, aircraft registration, flight sequence, and hours flown. It's not a big hassle, doesn't take much time but could save you money. You need this information anyway for you logbook.

Example cost sheets

Most flying schools will offer a course outline with expected flight hours, briefings etc to complete a certain licence or rating (whether it be PPL, CPL or an Instrument Rating).

Below is an example of a costing sheet you may find at a flying school for a student completing their commercial pilots licence with a breakdown of all hours required.

FLYING SCHOOL X

Course: Commercial Pilots Licence

Note: This outline details the costing and hours required from PPL to CPL (not training up to PPL)

Full Time: Approximately 12 months

Part Time: On your own time. 12 months minimum

HOURS	TYPE	RATE	TOTAL PRICE
60	C172 (Dual)	$330	$19,800
50	C172 (Solo)	$230	$11,500
5	Simulator (Dual)	$150	$750
40	Briefings	$80	$3,200
	Landing + Instrument fees		$400
	Fuel Levy		$500
	Theory manuals + Nav Charts		$400
	CPL Flight Test		$1950
74 hrs flight			**$38,500**

Any student requiring further training will be charged at the applicable rate as per the flying school rate sheet.

Flying schools will normally also have a list of prices for hire of both dual (with an instructor) and solo rates. An example is set out below. If you need to complete any hours above and beyond what is quoted for a particular licence, you can expect to pay the normal rate specified per hour.

Example of a flying school rate sheet:

FLYING SCHOOL X

FLYING SCHOOL RATES

SINGLE ENGINE AIRCRAFT	TAS	SEATS	SOLO	DUAL
Cessna 152	90	2	$200	$300
Diamond DA-20	110	4	$230	$330
Diamond DA-40	130	4	$240	$350
MULTI ENGINE AIRCRAFT				
Diamond DA-62	150	6	$450	$550
Beechcraft Baron	180	6	$500	$600
SIMULATOR				
Simulator			$100	$150
BRIEFINGS				
1 Hour Brief				$80

Conditions

1) The above rates do not include landing fees
2) The above rates do not include Airservices charges such as instrument approaches
3) Cancellation fees may occur if less than 24 hours' notice is given
4) The above rates may change without prior notice (fuel levy etc.)

TAS = True airspeed of the aircraft

SOLO = Price per hour for the plane by yourself

DUAL = Price per hour for the plane and instructor

VDO or Airswitch time

Flying schools charge by the hour. However there are two ways that the time is calculated. These are called either VDO or airswitch time. VDO is calculated from as soon as the engine is started until it is shutdown, whilst airswitch is from when the plane takes off until landing.

Factors to consider if a flying school charges based on VDO time is the amount of time it will take to taxi, perform pre-takeoff engine run-ups and before takeoff checklist items to takeoff and then the time taken to taxi back to the flying school after landing. This could take anywhere from 10-15 minutes (0.2 – 0.3 hours) extra each flight.

So you can compare apples with apples, if you are being charged on VDO time, you would have to add this amount of time onto the hourly cost of the plane being hired to compare it with airswitch time. If a flying school charges on VDO time, it should be cheaper than a school that charges on airswitch time to account for the longer period of time being charged for.

As an example; if a plane was being rented out at $200 an hour, a flight that lasted one hour in the air would cost exactly $200 if charged by airswitch, and a little more if rented out at VDO time to account for the taxi and runup time (for example, allowing for 15 minutes of taxi would cost $260 in total).

When determining which flying school to undertake your flying training with, make sure that you understand how they charge, by which of the above two types discussed above and compare it against other flying schools to ensure it is a competitive rate.

Additional flying training charges

On top of the basic cost per hour to hire an aircraft for the purposes of flying training, there are many more cost involved in obtaining a pilots licence. Some schools will include the below costs as part of their "packaged" costs for a PPL or CPL however it is worth checking with the school as to what is covered and what will need to be paid for additionally over the flying training component.

Note that the below costs are approximate, however they give a general guide of what's involved over basic flight hours. Note that as electronic flight bags (EFBs) are certified by CASA, there is not a requirement to purchase all the paper maps, Jeppessen charts, wizz wheels etc as has previously been the case.

You may be able to source some of these items through students at your school who do not need them anymore – for example a pilot that has completed their PPL licence may not require their theory books and you may be able to buy them for a reduced price. Another handy place to buy second-hand pilot items is off *Gumtree*.

Pre-training costs

Flying school uniform	$200
Navigation bag	$100-$200
Manuals	$150
Logbook	$30

RPL

Aircraft manual (if you cannot procure an electronic copy)	$50
Charts + Maps	$100
ERSA	$30
Pilot Headset	$300-$1000

PPL

Wizz wheel (Circular/sliding pilots calculator)	$50
PPL theory book	$60
Aircraft manual	$50

CPL

CPL theory books	$300-$500
Aircraft manual	$50
Text documents (AIP, CAO, CAAP, CAR)	$200-$300

(These are available online for free from the CASA/ASA websites)

What to expect during flying training

First Day

Once you have decided on which flying school to start training with and have enrolled, you may either have to wait for the pre assigned start date for your course so that you can start with other students or you may start training straight away. The first day will normally be a meet and greet where you will be introduced to all the staff and you will meet your instructor/s. They will also run you through general information about the flying school, safety, rules and what can be expected during your training. The school may have a syllabus of flights and training that you are expected to complete to obtain each rating a licence you wish to obtain.

Uniforms, theory books and charts

Depending on the school you may be issued or have to buy a uniform, navigation bag, aviation theory books and navigational charts. If you are purchasing a navigation bag to place all your manual and charts in when you're flying, I would highly recommend a soft bag over a hard one. You will find that the hard ones are too big to carry with you on the plane, especially during your first job where you will have a passenger occupying the front right seat and the bag will need to be placed between the seats. For making calculations in the air and for theory examinations, you will need the pilot's equivalent of a slide rule called a wiz wheel. I would also recommend buying a smaller, plastic one over a metal one that slides on a metal plate. These are easily stored in your shirt pocket.

You also don't need every single navigation chart, book and CASA regulation the first day you start training. You can save a couple of hundred dollars in amendment fees by buying them only when needed during your training. In terms of charts, you will only need what is called a WAC *World Aeronautical Chart*, a VTC *Visual Terminal Chart* and a VNC *Visual Navigation Chart*. Likewise you will probably not need every single CASA regulation on day one. You can download these from the CASA website and most information on the rules you will be using day to day are published in what is called the *VFR Flight Guide*, also available for free on the CASA website. Listed later in this book are apps that can be downloaded onto your tablet or iPad. Some of these allow you to buy a subscription for the maps and approach plates discussed above and may be a cheaper alternative. Confirm with your flight school whether they allow electronic copies of these documents before purchasing them however.

Normal flying day

Depending on the flying school and whether you are studying full time, you can expect to do a one hour briefing before every dual flight (dual flight meaning those that you do with your instructor). The briefing will recap the particular sequences and theory behind the flight you are about to commence. You will then be shown through a walk around before hopping in with your instructor. During the flight the instructor will demonstrate the flight sequence you are going to learn – for example with turns - he or she will first fly the turn, showing you the correct sequence before handing over the controls so that you can conduct the sequence yourself. You will do this a number of times to consolidate and fine tune the procedure.

After the flight you will then have a debriefing which will take anywhere for 30-60 minutes, depending on the amount of points that need to be covered.

A typical flight school syllabus

The syllabus for flying training is promulgated in a PDF document available from the CASA website called the day VFR flying syllabus. It's a bit of a dry read, however it explains in detail the syllabus that flying schools and consequently you, as a student, should follow to obtain the required flight experience for each licence. The document also specifies the standards that a s trident must achieve in each sequence in terms of competency, with these standards designed to make it clear to students what the exact testing and marking criteria are for each sequence.

Every pilot goes through the same first flights during their flying training. The table on the following pages is an example of what a typical pilot starting their training can expect to fly during their training up until their recreational licence.

Flight Sequence	Hours	Short Description
First Solo		
TIF	1.0	Optional flight. To decide whether you want to pursue aviation
Operation of effects and controls	1.0	Learn about the 3 controls of an aircraft – elevator, ailerons and rudder and their effects on the aircraft and on which axis
Straight and level	1.0	Learn to fly the aircraft at a certain altitude with wings level at differing power settings and speeds
Climbing and descending	1.0	Learn how to climb and descend the aircraft safely
Medium Level turns	1.0	Learn to conduct a coordinated turn at 30 degrees angle of bank
Circuits	1.0	Learn how to conduct a "circuit pattern" including the 4 legs of a circuit
Circuits	1.0	" "
Circuits	1.0	" "
Circuits	1.0	" "
Circuits (cross wind training)	1.0	Learn how to takeoff, land and fly a circuit during winds from either side of the aircraft
Circuits (cross wind training)	1.0	" "
First Solo	0.3	Conduct first solo (if ready by this stage)

Flight Sequence	Hours	Short Description
		Area Solo
Circuit consolidation	1.0	Consolidate the circuit work you have already completed
Solo Circuits	0.6	Conduct your second solo circuits – most likely more than one circuit including a touch and go
Circuit consolidation	1.0	Consolidate the circuit work you have already completed
Solo Circuits	1.0	Continued to consolidate circuit work on your own
Solo Circuits	1.0	" "
Forced Landings	1.0	Learn how to choose an area to land the plane if you are unable to restart the engine
Forced Landings	1.0	" "
Steep turns	1.0	Learn how to complete a coordinated turn at 45 and 60 degrees angle of bank
Advanced maneuvers	1.0	Consolidate all procedures you have learnt in the training area
Area consolidation	1.0	" "
Area solo check	1.0	Flight with your instructor to assess whether you are ready for your first area solo
Area solo	1.5	Conduct first area solo (if ready by this stage)

Flight Sequence	Hours	Short Description
		RPL
Precautionary search	1.0	Learn how to find and assess a safe landing area if you are forced to land due to darkness or bad weather
Basic instrument flying	1.0	Learn to how to fly the aircraft using only instrumentation
Instrument flying (limited panel)	1.0	Learn to how to fly the aircraft using only certain instrumentation
General area revision	1.5	Consolidate all procedures you have learnt in the training area
Area solo	1.5	Conduct another area solo
RPL check	1.5	Flight with your instructor to assess whether you are ready for your first area solo
Area solo	1.5	Conduct another area solo
RPL Test	1.0	Depending if ready by this stage

How flying schools structure flying lessons and courses

The flowchart on the following page outlines the steps required to obtain certain privileges, licences or ratings. Is should be read from top to bottom. Jobs on the right hand side of the chart explain where you might expect to be able to apply for a certain position with that amount of training completed, should you wish to choose that avenue.

Legend:

Heading

Optional

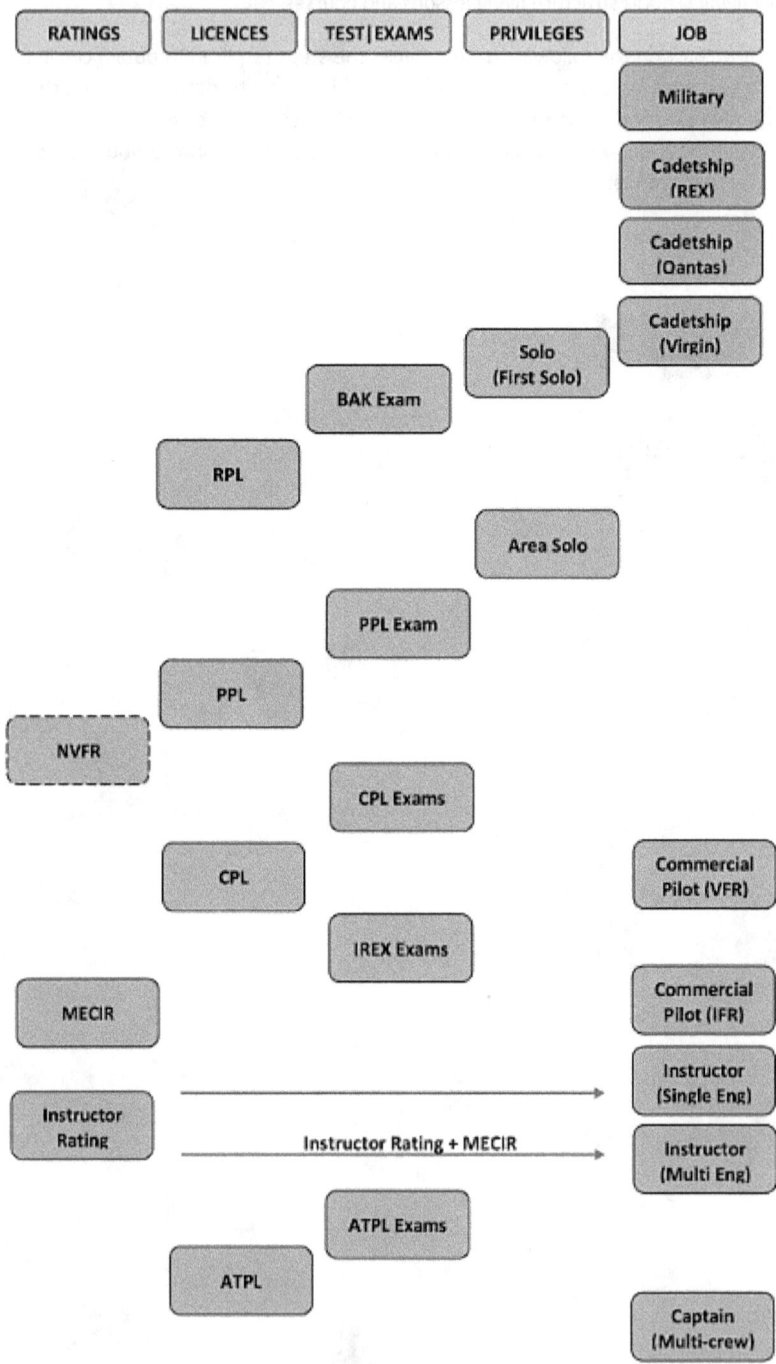

RATINGS	LICENCES	TEST|EXAMS	PRIVILEGES	JOB

Military

Cadetship (REX)

Cadetship (Qantas)

Cadetship (Virgin)

Solo (First Solo)

BAK Exam

RPL

Area Solo

PPL Exam

PPL

NVFR

CPL Exams

CPL

Commercial Pilot (VFR)

IREX Exams

MECIR

Commercial Pilot (IFR)

Instructor (Single Eng)

Instructor Rating

Instructor Rating + MECIR

Instructor (Multi Eng)

ATPL Exams

ATPL

Captain (Multi-crew)

Privileges, licences, ratings and endorsements explained

A **licence** means an examination whereby if successful, the pilot is given a particular licence which gives them certain privileges. For example, when a person undertakes their Private Pilots Licence, they have to do 3 things; complete all the required flight hours, a theory examination and flight examination. If they pass they receive their PPL.

The **privileges** then of the PPL is that that person may operate an aircraft anywhere in Australia with passengers on board under the rules of the PPL licence privileges set out what the licence or rating allows you to do with it.

A **rating** is like a licence but basically allows that pilot to operate under certain special conditions which an ordinary licence, whether it be a PPL or CPL doesn't allow. For example, if you would like to fly at night as a VFR pilot (without an instrument rating), you can complete a NVFR rating which allows you to fly at night. Another example is an instrument rating, which means that you are able to fly an aircraft without visual reference to the ground (in cloud or poor weather).

An **endorsement** relates to a specific aircraft feature and means that you must be taught how to correctly operate that feature. If for example an aircraft has a retractable gear/undercarriage (whereby the aircraft wheels are retracted after takeoff to reduce drag), you will need a "retractable gear" endorsement before flying that particular aircraft. Another example being a pressurization system; for aircraft that fly above 10,000 feet, the air is too thin to breathe normally and the air has to be "pressurized" by the engines and then fed into the aircraft cabin. This is a specific aircraft feature and also requires an endorsement.

How long can you expect to train for each licence?

The time taken to complete your flying training and gain different licences depends on a number of factors, included whether you are training full or part time. Most pilots will be able to achieve their commercial licence within a year and when also completing a multi-engine instrument rating or instructor rating, within one and a half to two years total.

The following diagram is an indication of how many flying hours (total) and how long it could take to get to that point in your training. (Excluding the MECIR and IR which show the amount of hours and time taken only for that specific rating).

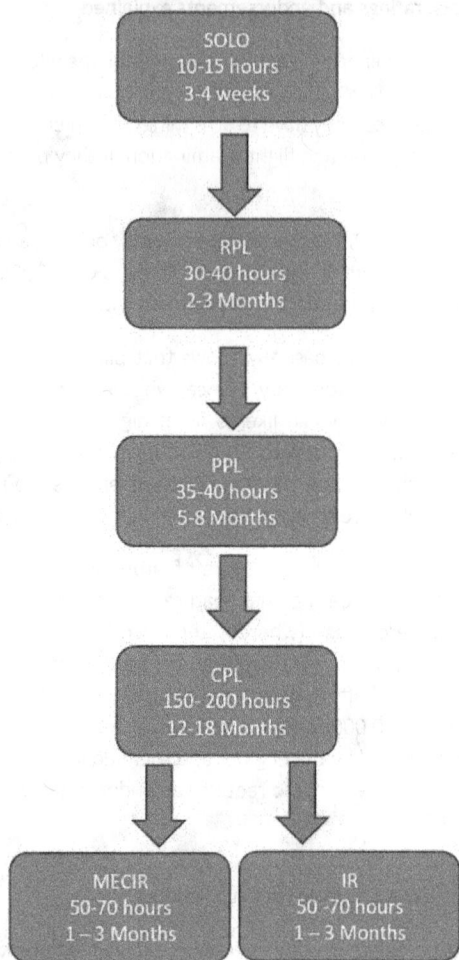

Pros and Cons of obtaining a MECIR vs Instructor Rating

Multi Engine Instrument Rating

MECIR job opportunities

Pros

✈ Once you gain your first job flying either scenic, parachute jumping or charter flying, you have the potential to build you hours up quite quickly.

✈ Airlines look advantageously on charter time and you may find that it leads to another company that flies twins or turboprops, which are usually the minimum requirements to be able to apply for an airline.

Cons

✈ Most charter jobs are based in remote and often small towns/communities. It may mean that you have to move quite often and to a small regional town or community.

Instructor Rating

Instructor job opportunities

Pros

✈ Most instructor jobs are based at flying schools and the majority of schools are based in cities or larger regional areas.

✈ You may receive a discount from the flying school you are working at for completing a multi-engine endorsement so that you can teach on those types of aircraft.

Cons

✈ Most airlines will look for experience on twin aircraft or twin turboprop aircraft. To gain that experience you will probably need charter experience eventually.

You should only complete your instructor rating if you are passionate about aviation and truly want to teach other people how to fly. Although it is another avenue to build hours with the possibly of not having to relocate remotely as with most charter jobs, you should not consider instructing as a career path to the airlines if the only reason you are doing it is for hour building.

Keeping a logbook

A pilot must keep a personal log book of all flight experience gained. Paper logbooks are able to be purchased from flight stores and Airservices Australia. Alternative you may decide to complete your logbook electronically via a phone or tablet app.

A logbook includes information such as endorsements and rating completed which are filled in at the front of the logbook and details of the flight including date, type of aircraft, registration and sequence flown as well as the number of hours gained in the appropriate column - day, night, single pilot, single engine, multi-engine.

As a pilot looking for their first job, you may find that it looks more professional to have a paper copy of your logbook to present to your future employer rather than a printed copy of an electronic logbook. The downside to this is that due to the technological advances, you may find it easier to use an app that you can enter all flight details. Some apps allow data to pre-populate over time and when you start flying as a career you may find that it is easier to use an app when you have many entries to complete each week.

Jeppessen and Airservices charts and subscriptions

When you start your instrument rating you will need to refer to instrument charts which specify the correct procedure to descend through cloud to an aerodrome for a safe landing, by navigating away from terrain in the area. Depending on the instrument aids at the aerodrome there may be different procedures. These procedures are printed and distributed by two companies, *Jeppessen* which is an American subsidiary of *Boeing* and *Airservices Australia*. Both companies produce these instrument charts however the data is displayed in a slightly different way. *Airservices Australia* documents are normally a cheaper alternative however when you move onto large and multi-crew aircraft or an airline your employer will usually expect or use *Jeppessen* plates. I decided to start with *Airservices Australia* charts during my instrument rating and first instrument flying job and then switch to *Jeppessen* plates at a later date. This saved me some money but also meant that I had to learn how to interpret the *Jeppessen* chart which wasn't an issue for other pilots who had been using them during their training. Your flying school may specify certain charts that you may need to use, however if not, you will need to weigh up whether the cost benefit outweighs the extra learning involved with changing charts at a later date.

The *OzRunways* app which will be discussed in detail later is the cheapest alternative over both the paper chart options discussed above, however you would need to check with your flying school whether electronic flight bag charts are able to be used during your instrument rating.

Using a flight simulator at home

Using a flight simulator on your personal computer is a great tool to become familiar with aircraft cockpits, instruments, navigation basics, and normal and emergency procedures. Using a flight simulator can help you save time and money in the real aircraft and can help improve your understanding of real world aviation. Given the processing power of today's computers means that flight simulator software for the home computer is impressively realistic.

There are two main flight simulation software packages that would be recommended for use at home, these being *Microsoft Flight Simulator* and *X Plane*.

In addition to the above programs, you will find that you will most likely be able to download a simulated model of the exact aircraft and its cockpit layout for your program.

Some of the things that a simulator may be able to help you in are as follows:

Cockpit preparation and checks

If you have a simulated model of the aircraft you are using at your flying school, you can practice checks and checklists in the flight simulator to make sure you know where everything is located in the cockpit and help save you money when the engine is running and you are paying for it.

Procedures

Although you can't practice everything in a computer flight simulator like a real aircraft, they can help you with new procedures you are learning or to consolidate old ones. For example say your next lesson at flying school was stalling. The procedure for a stall is as follows: apply full power, relax back pressure, use rudder to prevent further yaw, once the nose is below the horizon, roll wings level and recover to straight and level.

As you can see, the above procedure has quite a lot of steps involved and if you're practicing it for the first time in a real aircraft as the plane shudders and falls from the sky, it probably isn't going to be your best first attempt. However, if you were to practice the steps at home on flight simulator, you might have a better attempt in the aircraft at remembering all the steps in order.

Navigation

Flight simulator is really good for both instrument and visual navigation. If you are completing a navigation exercise for your private pilots licence, you can fly the same route beforehand on flight simulator. The graphics are realistic enough that you could "expect a mountain to be coming up on the right hand side at this point" and "I expect a lake to be coming up shortly". Flight simulators are also great tool for instrument flying skills as all the communication and navigation frequencies and navigational aids are exactly the same as in real life.

Minimum system requirements

The two latest versions of both programs are *Microsoft Flight Simulator X* and *X Plane 10*. The following are their **minimum** computer requirements to run:

✈ X Plane   Dual core | 2.5GHz | 4GB RAM | Video card with 1GB RAM
✈ Microsoft FSX   Single Core | 1 GHz | 512MB RAM | Video card with 32MB RAM

Cost

Assuming you have a computer that meets the above minimum requirements, the following approximate costs are involved in owning a simulator at home:

✈ Joystick $80 - $150
✈ Microsoft FSX $10 (online price)
✈ X Plane $80 (online price)

There is no substitute for the real thing, however as you can see, for the price of one or two hours of real flight lessons, you may be able to save time and money in the real aircraft by being able to practice checklists, upcoming procedures, navigation exercises or licence tests.

What will make you more employable once you have finished flying training

Apart from having enough hours, once you have finished flying training there a few things that you can do that will make you more employable over someone else. Some of these items are also mandatory before being employed as a pilot such as the dangerous goods certificate.

Most charter operators will require you to do many different tasks when you are employed as a pilot, not just fly aircraft. As a pilot you will need to be a jack of all trades. You will most likely help with checking in passengers and freight, answering telephone calls and making bookings, picking and dropping off passengers in a courtesy bus and cleaning of aircraft and hanger. You may even be required to mow the lawns!

Dangerous good certificate (mandatory)

There are different types of dangerous good certificates. It is a legal requirement that all pilots obtain a current dangerous goods **awareness** certificate. The awareness certificate basically means that you are educated in the subject of dangerous goods and how they relate to air carriage, not approval to accept dangerous goods.

Bus licence

Some scenic flight operators offer a courtesy bus to pickup and drop-off passengers from hotels and accommodation, and it may be the pilots job to drive the bus. Some companies run vans where a normal licence is require but larger operators do operate a small charter bus, where a light rigid licence (LR) is required to drive. Obtaining a LR licence can cost up to $500 so it is worth weighing up the cost versus whether it is required for the particular job you are seeking.

Aircraft experience

You are also more likely to be employed if you have previous experience on the types of aircraft that a company you may work for owns. If you have a choice between flying different type of aircraft during your training it would be advantageous to obtain hours on the same aircraft that are operated by charter and scenic companies in Australia. This normally only applies to multi engine aircraft as most single engine aircraft found at flying schools including single engine Cessna's, Pipers and Diamonds are not used for the purposes of charter or scenic work due to their size. Cessna 206's, Cessna 207's and Cessna 210's are most widely used for charter in the North of the country.

For example if you have a choice of flying either a Beechcraft Baron (6 seats) or a Beechcraft Duchess (4 seats and which is normally only used for teaching) you might want to considering completing either some or all of your training in the Baron as it is a very useful endorsement to have and is commonly used for charter work.

Do you require a NVFR Rating?

A Night VFR Rating is an optional rating you may complete during your training. A NVFR rating allows a pilot to fly an aircraft at night in the type of aircraft that the NVFR rating was flown in. That is, if you completed your NVFR rating in a single engine aircraft (which you most probably will), you will only be allowed to fly NVFR in a single engine aircraft.

A MECIR instrument rating allows you to fly at night time in an IFR rated aircraft anyway so you may be wondering whether it is necessary to complete a NVFR rating.

Most pilots that conduct charter or scenic flights gain the hours required for an ATPL easily apart from the night component. Because all scenic flights and passenger carrying charter flights in single engine pistons have to be flown during the day and most multi engine flights are flown in the daytime anyway, most pilots find it very hard to meet the 100 hours night required for an ATPL.

In the early part of your career, a NVFR rating is actually of more benefit than a MECIR. This is because most single engine aircraft are rated for VFR only – either Day VFR or Night VFR. Say for example you are working as a charter pilot in your first job and a flight comes up in the afternoon to drop off passengers and return empty. If you have a NVFR rating you would be able to fly those passengers to their destination, then return to base at nighttime, clocking up valuable night hours.

As you can see from the above, it is a win-win situation, in that you gain valuable night hours whilst the company benefits from being able to complete the charter. For this reason, you would be more employable than another pilot without a NVFR rating.

In addition to the above, whilst at flying school, I would recommend completing some or all of your multi engine instrument rating and possibly some of your CPL solo flights during night time. If the flying school doesn't allow you to hire an instructor at night for your MECIR flights outside of normal work hours, you might still be able to complete your CPL solo navigation flights at night. It costs no more money to do so and puts you in good stead for gaining the 100 hours at night required for the ATPL later on.

Do you require a MECIR before your first job?

Completing your multi-engine instrument rating during flying training or waiting until after you have obtained your first job as a pilot is an important factor to consider. It is also not necessary to complete your muti engine and instrument rating at the same time.

Although most pilots who decide to go down the hour building route of being a charter pilot complete their instrument rating during flying school after their commercial licence, there are many advantages to completing it after you have started flying in the real world.

✈ After gaining valuable flying hours as a commercial pilot, you would have also gained much more experience, which in turn will make completing your instrument rating that much easier.

✈ If you completed your instrument rating during flying school and now 12 months has passed since, you will need to renew it again, most likely with your own money. If you complete your instrument rating after working for 12 months, you miss out on one renewal process and the cost involved.

✈ If you are required by your company to have an instrument rating to be promoted and move onto different aircraft, you may be able to claim it against your taxable income.

The negatives of completing your instrument rating after gaining a flying job are the following:

✈ Although operating VFR aircraft, some general aviation operators, especially those in subtropical climates such as Cairns or Darwin during the wet season, would hire an instrument rated pilot over one that isn't. Someone with the same qualifications as you but with a MECIR is more employable.

✈ You're returning to base after completing a charter flight during the wet season and the weather starts to close. Although flying VFR, an instrument rating and the knowledge you have gained during training could save your life.

At a minimum it would be advantageous to complete your multi engine rating before starting work then completing your instrument rating at a later time when you are likely to move onto a twin engine aircraft flying IFR – for example your second flying job.

There are advantages and disadvantages to both, and there have been pilots that have completed their full multi engine instrument rating during flying training, only their multi engine rating or none at all until at a later date. The decision on when you want to complete your instrument rating depends on your personal preferences (including time and money at the time) and those of the company that you intend to work for.

Do you require your ATPL subjects before your first job?

It is very hard to complete your ATPL subjects (seven subjects in total) whilst you are working full time as a pilot. After a ten hour day of working and having to potentially wake up early again the next day for work, the last thing you want to do is study aviation. As disciplined as you may be, I know that each pilot I worked with at my first job that needed to study one or two subjects to finish off their ATPL examinations took nearly the entire year of studying on and off to eventually pass the exam.

If you have time during your flying training or just afterwards to complete at least most of the harder subjects, you will be in a far better position than trying to study all seven subjects whilst working full time. The subjects that are considered the hardest are flight planning, performance, aerodynamics and systems and navigation.

You have a rolling two years to complete all theory examinations for the ATPL. After that time, they start to expire at the date two years later than that which you completed them.

Self study vs theory course for ATPL subjects

The ATPL theory examinations are generally considered the most challenging exams completed during flying training. This is because they relate to jet airliner operations and include topics such as high speed aerodynamics, jet aircraft systems, high altitude metrology and long haul flight planning which are not covered or experienced during flying training.

You have two options for studying the ATPL subjects, either self-study or through a structured course taught by a theory instructor. CASA recommends that an average student should spend approximately 350 hours of study or 2-4 months of full time study to complete all ATPL examinations. For this reason, you should not consider self-studying the ATPL subjects unless you believe you have the tenacity, dedication and commitment to be able to study these subjects diligently by yourself outside of a structured classroom environment.

The four ATPL, examinations that are considered the hardest are navigation, flight planning, aerodynamics and performance and loading. Some pilot decide on a hybrid approach of studying these four harder subjects through an approved course whilst conducting the other three subjects during their own time.

CASA does not regulate theory schools like it does with flying organisations, so it would be best to conduct your own research to ensure the quality of the training you are receiving, much like the research you conducted when choosing a flying school. A large training organization that most pilots decide to use for the ATPL examinations is *Advanced Flight Theory* (AFT) located on the Sunshine Coast in Queensland. AFT offers both full time in classroom theory courses as well as distance learning courses which include all study notes and unlimited phone and email support.

Theoretical examinations and pass marks

The following chapter explains the different theoretical examinations and their associated subjects and pass mark. Examinations are conducted on a computer as a multiple choice questionnaire by a CASA exam system called *PEXO*, administered by an external company called *Assessment Services Pty Ltd (ASL)*.

Private	Time Allowed	Pass Mark
Private	3hrs 40min	70%
Commercial	Time Allowed	Pass Mark
Navigation	1hr 45min	70%
Meteorology	1hr 30min	70%
Human Factors	1hr 15min	70%
Air Law	2hrs	80%
Aerodynamics	1hr 30min	70%
Aircraft General Knowledge	1hr 30min	70%
Ops, Performance and Planning	2hrs 30min	70%
ATPL	Time Allowed	Pass Mark
Air Law	1hr 30min	80%
Human Factors	1hr 15min	70%
Meteorology	1hr 30min	70%
Navigation	1hr 30min	70%
Flight Planning	3hrs	70%
Performance and Loading	2hrs 30min	70%
Aerodynamics and Systems	1hr 30min	70%
IREX	Time Allowed	Pass Mark
IREX	3hrs 30min	70%

What type of first flying jobs are there for prospective pilots?

There are many different types of flying jobs available to pilots with a commercial licence. The most common ones are becoming an instructor and teaching people how to fly or charter or scenic flights.

Most instructing jobs will be in capital cities and larger towns as this is where flying schools are based, whereas charter and scenic flight positions are normally found in smaller, regional areas or Aboriginal communities.

Other type of first jobs available to prospective pilots include skydiving and survey work.

Finding your first job

If you are looking for an instructing job, make sure that you impress the current school you are training at. Some schools may offer as part of the course a position as an instructor at their school, however this is not always the case. Talk to the instructors at your flying school, make sure you are on time or early for your lessons and perhaps speak to the Chief Pilot or owner about your interest in working for the flying school once you have finished your training.

If you have any friends including those from flying training that already work in the industry, ask them to question whether they know of any leads, or if the company they are currently working at is hiring.

If you are training for the career path of first becoming a charter or scenic pilot, you will probably find out very quickly that you will not be able to find a job by sending out resumes and calling operators. On paper most pilots look the same - straight out of flying school with a fresh CPL, 200-250 hours, looking for their first job, living on the other side of the country. If you do speak to any operations or reception person on the other end of the phone, don't be rude or discouraged if they aren't warm back to you.

As discussed above, most first jobs are to be found remote - that is either Far North Queensland, Western Australia or the Territory. The people that get the jobs are the ones that are living in the places where the job openings might happen. If an charter company needs a pilot - chances are they needed them to start work yesterday. You may have to pack up your life and move with the prospect of hopefully obtaining a job. I moved to Kununurra, lived in the backpackers, worked at the hotel for 4 months, religiously went into all the flying operators each week and introduced myself, cleaned planes for free and was told that there were no current job openings. A day later I received phone call from the Chief Pilot telling me to come in that day for a check flight. The day after that I started work and two days later I was conducing my own scenic flights with paying passengers.

In terms of relocating yourself, car and your belongings there are two options. The first is driving yourself with your car packed with belongings to wherever you are hoping to obtain a job. If you are looking somewhere in Cairns, Darwin or Broome, you may find that placing your car on a freight train is cheaper than the associated costs of driving yourself (fuel and hotel). It will probably be the first time you have moved away from home and the thought of leaving home for the first time for an elusive flying job in the middle of nowhere can be quite daunting.

You will ideally want to be looking for a job at the end of the wet/start of the dry season. Scenic work does drop off during the wet season with charter work only slightly decreasing as unsealed road closures cut off communities and town from the outside road by flood water, needing to be resupplied by air.

In terms of accommodation, your best bet when you arrive at the place you are looking for a job is to check into the local backpackers. Depending where you are, you do not want to be signing any six or twelve months leases just yet as you don't even know if you will have a job at this stage. In places like Kununurra you will find that it is nigh on impossible to find any other place to stay anyway with accommodation so tight during the dry season.

Don't expect to find your first job straight away. It does take some people weeks or even months to find their elusive first job. Some people will need to apply and work a job at either the local pub, stacking shelves at the supermarket or working at the petrol station for a few months before they are eventually offered a checkride with one of the operators in the area.

You may be asked if you can help out and wash planes and clean the hanger. This is not a question, as your potential future employer is assessing your willingness and how much you want the job. You will not be paid nor will it automatically mean that you have a job.

Where should you look for your first aviation job?

Below is a list of towns where you may be able to find a first job. The diagram below is definitely not an exhaustive list of all places to find a first job, but an indication of where most jobs could be found.

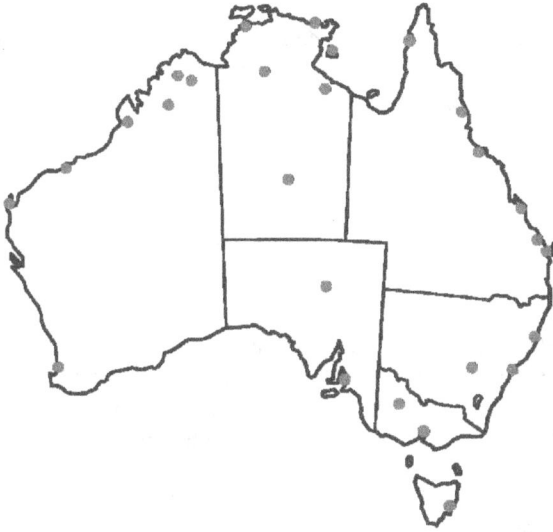

Charter operators

All capital cities (although most will require more than minimum hours) Kununurra, Broome, Exmouth, Cairns, Darwin, Katherine, Jabiru, Lajamanu, Townsville, William Creek, Port Hedland, Wyndham, Borolooola, Halls Creek, Alice Springs, Emerald, Weipa

Scenic operators

Kununurra, Broome, Exmouth, Cairns, Darwin, Katherine, Jabiru, Townsville, William Creek

Sky diving

All capital cities, Gold Coast, Cairns, Darwin, Bryon Bay, Rainbow Beach, Coffs Harbour etc.

There are quite a lot of sky dive operators through Australia. A full list of drop zones within Australia can be found at the Australian Parachute Federation website at:

www.apf.asn.au/APF-Zone/Skydive-Info/Drop-Zone-List

Survey work

Survey work is conducted throughout Australia. There are many aerial survey operators, most of them use a variety of different aircraft depending on the mission however some do operate C210's and other small single engine piston aircraft. You will find that a lot of survey operators require more than just the minimum amount of hours that a CPL student will have, and thus may not be obtainable as a first flying job.

Websites for job searching

www.afap.org.au

The *Australian Federation of Air Pilots* is a professional association that promotes the interest of pilots within Australia. They have a dedicated page on their website that allows you to peruse jobs that employers have posted online. The operators are not affiliated with the AFAP in any way so it is best to conduct your own research about any jobs that you are considering applying for.

www.pprune.org

A forum, worldwide with a large Australian presence, right through from air traffic controllers, people learning to fly and Captains of large jet aircraft. Although they don't advertise pilot jobs there are a large amount of threads with posts containing a lot of information for prospective pilot and details about first flying jobs. If you create an account you can post your own threads and ask people about certain locations and jobs and gain information from people that have "been there and done that".

I found my first flying job by starting a thread and asking where I should look for my first flying job. Most people agreed at the time that Kununurra in WA was the way to go and so I moved to WA and obtained a flying job a few months later.

www.pilotcareercentre.com

Although not Australian based, they do advertise information relating to Australian aviation operators with lots of information including names of recruitment personnel to address CV's to, hiring status, minimum requirements and email addresses.

www.airportjobseekers.com

Contains a list of aviation jobs throughout Australia.

New Zealand

New Zealand is also a place for job searching for first time pilots. Although a lot of New Zealand pilots come to Australia in search of jobs, there are a variety of scenic, charter and skydiving opportunities available in New Zealand. More so than Australia however, you will have to move to New Zealand before an operator will even offer the chance of a checkride or interview. You will most likely not have any response to a resume you send to flying companies in New Zealand if you are living in Australia.

Working overseas for your first job

Some jobs are available overseas for new commercial pilots. Although it would be recommended to try and find a job within Australia, the following places around the world have been known to take low hour pilots.

Africa

Botswana, Namibia, Tanzania, Zambia, Malawi, Uganda

Asia

Jakarta, India

Resume

Applying for a job, especially a first pilot job straight out of flight school involves selling yourself. One rule for first time pilots is to try and keep your resume to one page. Operators get literally hundreds of resumes each year. It is for this reason that your resume must be competitive, and offer your prospective future employer something that either stands out or offers above every other qualified pilot looking for their first job. Chances are that every prospective pilot will have approximately the same qualifications and number of hours straight out of flight school as one another. What is the difference between two pilots – both having the same qualifications and hours. That is the question you need to answer and present to a future employer.

In all, you need to distinguish yourself from the other dozens of prospective, job searching pilots. The three golden rules of a resume for a first time pilot are as follows:

- ✈ Try and keep your resume to one page, 2 maximum. It should be succinct and to the point.
- ✈ Make sure that your resume is free of both spelling and grammatical errors. This one is common sense however you will be surprised how many prospective job hunters present resumes that are not.
- ✈ Be easy to read in a well laid out format.

Presentation and checkride

The key to any job, especially in the aviation industry, is to network, network, and network. The aviation industry in Australia is small, and the line "it's not what you know, it's who you know" couldn't be any more accurate. I was offered a job from an operator in Broome whilst working as a waiter at a hotel in Kununurra because I noticed a patron reading an aviation magazine and I asked him if he was a pilot. He introduced himself as the Chief Pilot of a large charter company in Broome. He gave me his number and when he was in town a week later we had an informal interview and I was offered a full time job on the spot. Although I didn't take the job because I was offered a full time flying position in Kununurra, it goes to show that aviation is a small community.

The only way that the operators are going to know that you are in town and looking for a job is to visit them in person. When you do so, you want to make sure you look the part. It might be the outback and stinking hot, but first impressions last and make all the difference. I will never forget arriving at a scenic operator's reception in dress jeans and a nice looking black shirt. The other candidates wore similar clothing. The only person that got the job was the one dressed in a business suit with tie. He had a few hundred hours more than us, but the Chief Pilot at the time did make a point of telling us that he had dressed the part. This is your only chance to make a first impression, so make sure it counts. If you are going to wear a pilot shirt, make sure that you leave your bars and wings off. If the chief pilot is unable to meet with you at that instant, kindly talk to the receptionist or the line pilot behind the desk, stating that you have just moved to town, are looking for your first job, and would like to schedule an appointment with the Chief Pilot.

You may be offered a check-ride at some stage. Depending on the company, it might be an informal, start-up, taxi-out and a few circuits with the Chief Pilot in the right hand seat, or it could start with an oral examination with some basic questions and the flight consisting of taxi, take-off, forced landings, steep turns and circuits. The check-flight will most likely be conducted in an aircraft that is quite a lot heavier than what you have been used to flying during your training, and one that you have never flown before.

Depending on where you have set yourself up, don't be disheartened if the company you have been successful in obtaining a job with want to send you remote or to an Aboriginal community. Some charter operators have more than one base, with the smaller and more remote bases being crewed by new pilots. Remember that your job is only half of the experience. The other pilots that you work with remote will probably be the closest friends you will have for the rest of your life, and the experiences you will have both in the air and on the ground will be remembered for a long time after you leave general aviation.

Simple interview tip and pointers

There is a plethora of interview preparation books and an unlimited supply of information available on the internet regarding interviews. There are also many books written specifically for airline interviewing techniques. This book is not intended as preparation for your interview, however I have complied some simple preparation tips, interview etiquette and how to conduct yourself.

Most smaller companies which employ pilots with low hours will be more informal in their hiring process, and instead of an interview, you may be shown around the company office and introduced to other employees before conducting a check flight and possible quick interview. Some of the tips below may seem common sense however you'll be surprised how many people fail interviews due to lack of preparation after they have spent upwards of $100,000 learning to fly.

Pre interview preparation

➤ Study all limitations including speeds, weights and systems of the aircraft that you have flown either at flight school, or your first job if you are preparing for your second flying job.

➤ Know about the company you are applying for including the aircraft they operate and where they fly to. If the company operates different bases know their locations too. You should have a basic understanding of their operation and also the remote bases that you might be relocated to.

➤ Plan your trip to wherever the operator you are visiting is based so that you arrive on time, and preferable about 10-15 minutes early.

Presentation

➤ Make sure you are clean shaven prior to the interview. This includes a conservative haircut.

➤ Cover any visible tattoos.

➤ Carry backup paper and copies of your resume, licence and medical. It may also pay to have these as an electronic copy on an app such as *Dropbox* or *iCloud* so that you can email these straight through if required.

➤ Depending on the company and location you should wear a plain white shirt with black pants and shoes. If you are applying for a job in places such as Darwin, Kununurra, Broome you should be able to get away without wearing a jacket due to the heat. Under no circumstance should you wear your pilot shirt with epaulettes/rank-sleeves fitted.

The interview

➤ First impressions last, when you meet the interviewer, whoever that may be, the chief pilot, owner or senior base pilot, make sure you make eye contact and shake their hand firmly.

➤ Don't sit down before your interviewer has taken their seat first.

➤ Do not slander anyone or any company during the interview process. There will be time for this after you are employed.

➤ At the end of the interview, try and use the interviewers name when the interview ends and you both farewell each other.

Airline Specific Interview Tips

The above interview tips apply to any interview you may be offered. Most airline interviews however will be behavioral based, whereby you will be asked approximately 6-8 questions relating to previous life and job experiences and how you dealt with those situations. These questions normally start with "tell us about a time..." whereby you then have to explain a past experience and how you handled it. Example questions include situations such as:

"Tell us about a time you saved the day"
"Tell us about a time you had to work to a deadline and how you managed your time effectively"
"Tell us about a time you had to deal with someone difficult and how you handled the situation"
"Tell us about a time you turned a negative situation into a positive one"

These types of behavioral questions are based on the premise that how you dealt with a situation in the past can be a good indicator of how you would handle a similar situation in the future.

With behavioral based questions such as these, it is worth having a few scenarios that you have though through beforehand that you can talk about to fit the particular question they have asked.

The best way to answer these types of behavioural questions is using the *STAR* technique. STAR stands for Situation, Task, Action, Result, and this is how you should structure your answers. Using this strategy is very helpful.

Situation

This is where you explain the situation you're going to apply to this question. You explain to the interviewers the situation/scenario, being as specific as possible so that they can build a picture in their head of what your situation was. Remember that some of the people on the interview panel may have no piloting experience.

You then continue answering by explaining the task at hand, what you were doing, and perhaps other team members that lead to a certain situation.

Action

This is where you describe what action you and/or your team took to meet the challenge or situation that you were in.

Result

Whether the outcome was either positive or negative, you will then explain what the end result of the situation was. If you have described the action you took to resolve the challenge you met and you showed the interviewers that you used good communication, teamwork, applied logical thinking to the problem etc, they will not be interested in the end result.

Wrap-up

A final tip which is not included in the original STAR technique, but is good to include at the end of your answer is to repeat the initial question that was asked of you, which wraps up the answer to their question nicely.

A worked example

As you read through the response below, try and notice the different parts of the STAR format contained within the answer. The interview panel asks you the question "tell us about a time you turned a negative situation into a positive situation?". You have formulated a couple of scenarios, at home prior to attending the interview so you're not trying to recall situations on the fly. One of the scenarios you prepared using the STAR technique was about a stressful day a work where you had a delayed departure due to an aircraft going unserviceable and then departed an hour late after you got a new airframe. You then explain this situation to the interviewers:

"When I was working in Darwin last year on the Cessna 404 which is a single pilot, twin engine aircraft, I was rostered to conduct a charter flight to Bathurst Island in the wet season. As I was working on the weekend, we didn't have the usual office and check in staff whom would help load the plane and check in the passengers, so I had to manage my time effectively to check in passengers, load their bags myself and depart on time. Once all the passengers were on board I started both engines. One of the pre-taxi checks of the engine failed on the right engine and as it was a no-go item I had to shutdown the aircraft and explain the situation to the passengers. I escorted the passengers back to the office and explained to them that I would be calling operations to see what other planes were available. I offered them water whilst they waited and then called the ops manager who informed that another 404 was available although it hadn't flown that day and thus would need engine runups prior to loading passengers. One of the other pilots was finishing work for the day so I asked for his assistance in unloading the passenger's bags which I ran up the new aircraft. When I returned, I informed the passengers that I just had to load their bags on the new aircraft and I'd come collect them in about 5 minutes. After loading the bags I escorted the passengers back out to the plane and we departed an hour late. When we landed half an hour later I thanked the passengers for their patience. Although late, the passengers were appreciative that I had kept them informed of the situation and had seen that I was working by myself with little support. I was able to as the help of a fellow pilot which lessened the delay further. This was a situation where I was able to turn a negative outcome into a positive one.

Did you notice the different aspects of the STAR process in the answer above? The **situation** is when you're describing the scenario – flying in Darwin, on the weekend on a Cessna 404 out to Bathurst Island. The **task** is checking in the passengers, loading their bags, working with little support on the weekend. The **action** is what you did after the engine pre-taxi checks failed and how you handled the situation. The **result** – even though you were late, the passengers were appreciate and they understood the situation and were happy that you kept them informed of the delay throughout with good communication. You also employed teamwork with the help of a fellow pilot which reduced the delay further. **Wrap-up** – notice how the answer ends with repeating to interviewers question to further solidify your answer and provide a succinct summary of how this answers their question.

Your first job. The good and the bad

Instructor

As an instructor you could expect to work approximately 5 days a week, generally from Monday through Friday. You will be instructing a number of different students at different levels throughout their training. You will normally be required to give the student a briefing on the flight sequence to be flown and the theory associated with the flight. The flight, depending on the sequence flown, whether circuits or a dual navigation exercise as part of their PPL training could last anywhere from one to four hours. After the flight, you will then conduct a debriefing with your student. This addresses the positives and negatives of the flight and points that the student should consolidate for the next flight. Some busy flying schools will have instructors complete a three hour navigation exercise in the morning and then two one hour lessons in the afternoon.

Charter/Scenic Pilot

Your first job will be the position where you have the greatest stick and rudder control over an aircraft. As you start moving onto larger aircraft that are equipped with autopilot, you will be not only encouraged but even made to use this as part of company operating procedures. Just because you are in the middle of nowhere, it doesn't mean that you should lax on your flying skills, airmanship or judgment. Don't use the outback as an excuse to do anything illegal or life threatening. Low passes, beat-ups and formation flying are only a few things that most general aviation pilots have done during their first few hundred hours of flying for their first company. If you make a bad name for yourself either with the company or CASA then you will find it very hard to find another job after you lose your first one you tried so hard to obtain.

Most general aviation aircraft have been around a lot longer than you have. They are old and have many hours on the airframe and engine. They need to be treated with care and respect. Failures will happen and you need to be prepared for such an occurrence. Whether it is a cockpit instrument, or something more serious such as a fuel pump or engine seizure, mechanical failures are more likely to occur during your first few years of flying.

Some operators will ask you to bend the rules. Not all will, but it is the outback and profit is made by your employer being able to squeeze out as much as they can from yourself and the plane. Whether it is to extend your duty time when you have no more left, to carry an extra passenger that may push you over weight or fly back right on last light where you will land after the sun has set, you will be pressured into doing a number of things. It is your first job, and yes your job possibly can be filled by another pilot, however if it doesn't look or feel right it probably isn't. The three main things that you will may find yourself being pressured into is flying over your legally required flight and duty limits, flying overweight and flying a plane that has an unrectified maintenance issue.

The weather can change quickly in the outback of Australia. The dry season is docile, however visibly can reduce to zero with the amount of smoke trapped by the inversion layer during that time of the year. During the wet season, the weather is unpredictable and can change quite quickly. As a first time pilot flying VFR, you do not want to be relying on your instrument flying skills. Don't get caught out by bad weather such as unforecast fog and thunderstorms. Always check your NOTAMs and weather thoroughly and take the required amount of fuel required plus more. The two largest pressures for a VFR pilot once in the air are fuel and daylight.

A storm builds quickly as we pass alongside

Remember that from your perspective, the whole point of your first flying job is to obtain hours and experience. From an employer's point of view, you are there to make the company money. Depending on the company you could be expected to work anywhere for 5-6 days a week. You will not just be a pilot but much, much more. Jobs such as administration, check in, answering phones, cleaning of planes and hanger and picking up and drop off of passengers are usual before and after flying chores.

Small, general aviation companies do not have the backing nor money like the airline industry. To save money they employ the minimum amount of staff required to operate and thus, as pilot, you will be a jack of all trades. A normal job as a charter or scenic pilot may start with a 4am wakeup, before donning your pilot uniform and heading to the airport. Depending on the company, you may be required to complete a pre-flight daily inspection, refuel, pick up passengers, check them in and weight them before taking to the air. After the flight, you may be required to drop off passengers again before completing another preflight and refuel before flying again. You may fly up to eight hours day, between four to eight sectors, all in a twelve hour day which is interspersed with the afore mentioned jobs of plane washing, hanger cleaning and admin work.

The amount of duty hours that your employer may ask you to log may be questionable in that you may be pressured to record less hours than you actually work during the week. It may not be uncommon for a pilot to work 6 days a week as the minimum amount of days off required as per the Government award for a general aviation pilot is one per week.

Some jobs like this may have you working a lot whereas others there may be very little flying with some people only gaining 200-300 hours of flying over the course of a year.

You may also be offered a part time or casual flying position. Don't let this deter you as you may find that the position turns into a full time job if another pilot leaves or if work ramps up. Casual and part time positions can occur in parachuting and scenic operations to account for the seasonal nature of the flying required.

Above all else, just remember to not give up on your dream. You have spent countless hours, time, effort and money to get to where you are. Many pilots have dropped out of the industry before obtaining their first job, some also much later in their career. It's not an easy industry, it required, tenacity, dedication and true grit. If it was too easy then it wouldn't be so enviable and a career where people say "Oh I wish that I had become a pilot".

Unloading 500kg of freight in the Kimberley

Must have items

There are a few things that every pilot that travels remote should have. The first thing being intangible and is attitude. Come with a willingness to learn, an open mind and an outlook of what you can do to help out the company. Proving that you want to learn will get your foot in the door.

You should carry a few things with you in your nav bag. The first is a handheld GPS. Most general aviation single engine aircraft will not have a built in GPS. Even if they do, it is best to carry a backup. In the middle of the outback with smoke reducing visibility to 10km it is always good to have a GPS to confirm tracking, especially when everything looks the same for miles on end. Be sure to carry spare batteries and have them handy when you need them too.

In lieu of a dedicated GPS unit, I detail a few applications that you can install on your iPad or phone in a later section of this chapter. Some of these allow you to have the aircraft GPS position overlayed on an aeronautical chart of your choice.

You should also have a spare torch in your bag. Not only is it a CASA requirement, but older aircraft can have electrical issues. When flying at night, take it out of your nav bag and place it somewhere within easy reach. The last thing you want to do when the lights fail on takeoff is to be fumbling around in your nav bag looking for it. Pilots have died from their cockpit lights failing on takeoff at night. A green or red lamp is the best as it does not destroy your night vision and LED's are the cheapest and most reliable.

You will be working up to twelve hours a day with little time to eat or drink. It is important to stay hydrated and to eat during the day due to the temperatures and operating environment you will be working in. I remember seeing the thermometer gauge inside my 207 hit 70° Celsius after landing at *Kalamburu* in the Kimberley. If you don't want to carry around a full lunchbox you can use a hydration backpack with some form of nonperishable sustenance such as muesli bars in your nav bag.

A mobile phone can be a lifesaver when flying in the outback (your employer will probably expect you to have one regardless for being contactable when on standby etc). Depending where you are looking for a job, check the coverage maps of your current provider to check that they will work. There is only one mobile phone service provider in Australia that offers superior service and is guaranteed to work, especially in those communities that only have their reception towers.

You should also pack sunscreen, as you can get burnt quite quickly working out in the sun for long periods of time when loading and cleaning planes.

Mistakes and errors

If you are unsure of anything during your first job it is always best to seek the opinion or advices of a more senior pilot or your chief pilot. As a low hour pilot you will inevitable have questions and your senior peers and boss are there to help, guide and mentor you through this first job. Chances are they have asked a similar question in the past. As careful as you may be however, we all make mistakes. This is what makes us human. During your first job you will make a mistake or error at some stage. Whether it is a small error or a massive stuff up it is best to explain to your boss (either your Senior Base Pilot, Chief Pilot or owner) before they find out themselves. As long as it is not a negligent or deliberate mistake they will probably understand the situation, having probably been there or in a similar position themselves in the past. The worst thing you can do is try and cover up your mistake on the premise that you may lose your job. Either your employer or CASA may find out about it and it will be a completely different story.

Make sure that you do a thorough walk around of the aircraft after all the passengers or cargo are loaded and before you are about to start engines. Common errors include leaving the pitot covers attached, cargo doors unlocked, wheel chocks still in place or clipboard or phone on the tailplane. A quick walk around can ensure that these do not happen to you.

If you are parking in a confined spare such as an apron without much room make sure that you taxi slowly. There is always no excuse for a taxiing accident and you will most likely lose your job. Likewise be careful of where your propwash is directed. Never try and point the tail of your aircraft towards an open hanger or the open doors of another aircraft.

Useful phone and tablet apps

OzRunways

www.ozrunways.com

OzRunways is an app that runs on both iOS and android tablets. It is what's called an EFB or Electronic Flight Bag. Before EFBs, pilots had to carry all of their maps, charts and navigational books in paper copy. *OzRunways* allows pilots throughout Australia to carry a tablet with an EFB installed, as a substitute for carrying all the required charts and navigational data in paper form. *OzRuways* not only contains all the navigational data that you require but it also places your GPS position on a moving map. The maps can be overlaid with visual or instrument charts. It also allows you to flightplan and obtain weather and NOTAM briefing information. A very similar EFB to *OzRunways* is an application called *AvPlan*. You should also consider *AvPlan*, however *OzRunways* is the most widely used app by Australian pilots.

LiveATC Air Radio

The LiveATC app provides a quick and easy way to listen to real time conversations between pilots and air traffic control. Multiple countries, airports and different frequencies (such as ground, tower, approach etc) can be selected.

During flying training this app can be handy as you can listen to correct radio calls made by pilots at different phases of flight.

FlightRadar24 – Flight Tracker

With this app you can find any aircraft that is currently in the sky (except those that aren't fitted with an electronic device called ADS-B). It contains all data about that flight including current speed, altitude, flightpath, transponder code and much more.

NAIPS

(Only available for iOS)

NAIPS is an app which allows the user to easily access weather and NOTAM briefings. It also allows the pilot to submit flight plans, GPS/RAIM predictions, view different weather charts and much more. OzRunways includes most of the features of NAIPS however if you don't have OzRunways this is a very handy app to have, especially for first time pilots.

Many aerodromes within Australia provide the current weather via an automatic weather station. This is then converted into information that is then displayed to a pilot in a defined format, including cloud height and type, temperature, pressure, rainfall and wind. This information is also available by phoning the phone number associated with the automatic weather station at the aerodrome. This free app has a list of all phone numbers and can automatically dial the automated weather station of many airports within Australia.

Tax deductions as a pilot

As a pilot you are able to claim many tax deductions through the course of your normal flying career. As a new time pilot you may be unaware of the items which you are able to claim on your annual tax return and so, I have created a list of items which are listed below that you may be able to claim. These items are used in the course of your normal employment as a pilot, which will reduce your taxable income for the financial year.

Please note that the following is a guide only and you should either check with your accountant or the ATO (Australian Taxation Office) to determine which items below are applicable to your situation. The ATO website has a section dedicated specifically to deductions claimable by pilots. Also note that if your employer provides you with any of these items or an allowance for an item (such as a phone allowance), you will not be able to claim those items on your tax return.

You can only claim the below items during flying training if you are employed as a pilot within the same financial year that you finish flying training and use them as part of your normal flying duties.

- ✈ Sunscreen - where it is used to combat the effects of dehydration due to flying
- ✈ Moisturizer – same as sunscreen
- ✈ Sunglasses
- ✈ Uniforms - non-generic only (can't claim black socks etc)
- ✈ Phone - most general aviation companies will require you to be contactable 24/7 and thus you will be able to claim the full or a portion of your phone plan as part of employment – check with your accountant
- ✈ Internet - a portion of your internet connection maybe tax deductible
- ✈ Computer/laptop - for the purposes of checking weather, company emails etc
- ✈ Charts and manuals - Any charts, manuals and associated amendments or subscriptions to Ozrunways or Jeppessen required in the normal course of your employment
- ✈ Pilot logbook
- ✈ Union/professional association fees
- ✈ Medical examination - Class 1 medical
- ✈ ASIC fee
- ✈ Aviation related magazines - for example *Australia Aviation* and *Australian Pilot* - however only if you can justify to the ATO that the reading of these magazines increases your aviation knowledge directly applicable to your employment
- ✈ Watch – The ATO specifies that a watch cannot be claimed however the CAO's state that a pilot must own and wear a watch during his or her employment so it would be best to check with your accountant
- ✈ Uniform washing and dry cleaning - You are able to claim any dry cleaning and costs associated with washing your uniforms. For the purpose of calculating washing and drying costs, the ATO uses the following "reasonable cost basis": $1 per load or $0.50 per load if a mixed load of work and non-work clothing is washed. For example, if you wash your uniform twice weekly, you could claim up to $104 per annum (2 washes x 52 weeks X $1 per wash). Note: the maximum amount you may claim for washing of your uniform without providing receipts is $150 per annum.

In addition to the above items, you may be able to claim depreciation on any assets that you use during the course of your employment such as sunglasses, laptop, phone etc.

Deducting flying training and courses

If you complete your instrument rating or ATPL theory subjects before gaining your first flying job you will not be able to claim these against your taxable income. If however you begin training and then complete for example your instrument rating or ATPL theory subjects (which run upwards of $20,000 for the instrument rating and $4000-$6000 for the ATPL theoretical examinations) you may be able to claim these as part of your income as you need to obtain the required knowledge to progress through your career (for example, obtain an upgrade to IFR, multi-engine aircraft or multi crew turbine Captain upgrade).

I recommend conducting your own due diligence before claiming any deduction, and I strongly advise speaking to a qualified tax accountant before claiming a large deduction such as an instrument rating, multi-engine rating or ATPL subjects to determine whether they are closely related enough to your currently and or near foreseeable future employment to be either full or partially claimable.

Where next?

After working with your current employer building hours you may be asking "what next?" You may either want to stay with your current employer or you may want to look for a different job to advance your career. Reasons for leaving may include that that company doesn't have any larger aircraft that you are able to progress onto, having gained enough hours to apply for certain cadetships, or the company you are working for is based remote and you would like to move to a larger town.

Generally, after you have obtained around 1000 hours total time, you will be employable at a company which operates twin engine aircraft. You may find however that you have to fly single engine aircraft again for a certain period of time at this new company before you will be able to progress onto a twin.

If you have been working as an instructor, you may want to continue to teach, or upgrade to become a grade two instructor, or you may have the experience required to fly a turbine aircraft, either single or multi crew.

Progression through aircraft and jobs

Below is a flowchart of what type of aircraft and what type of jobs you could potentially progress through during your hour building.

```
┌─────────────────────┐
│ Single Engine Piston │
│ Charter|Scenic|Instructing │
└─────────────────────┘
        │         └──────►┌─────────────┐
        │                 │  Cadetship  │
        ▼                 └─────────────┘
┌─────────────────────┐
│ Multi Engine Piston │
│ Charter|Scenic|Instructing │
└─────────────────────┘
        │         └──────►┌─────────────┐
        │                 │  Cadetship  │
        ▼                 └─────────────┘
┌──────────────┐  ┌──────────────┐
│  Turbine F/O │  │   Turbine    │
│ (Multi Crew) │  │ (Single Crew)│
└──────────────┘  └──────────────┘
    │      │              │
    ▼      ▼              ▼
┌──────────────┐ ┌────────────┐ ┌────────────┐
│Turbine Captain│ │ Airline F/O│ │ Airline F/O│
│ (Multi Crew) │ └────────────┘ └────────────┘
└──────────────┘
    │
    ▼
┌────────────┐
│ Airline F/O│
└────────────┘
```

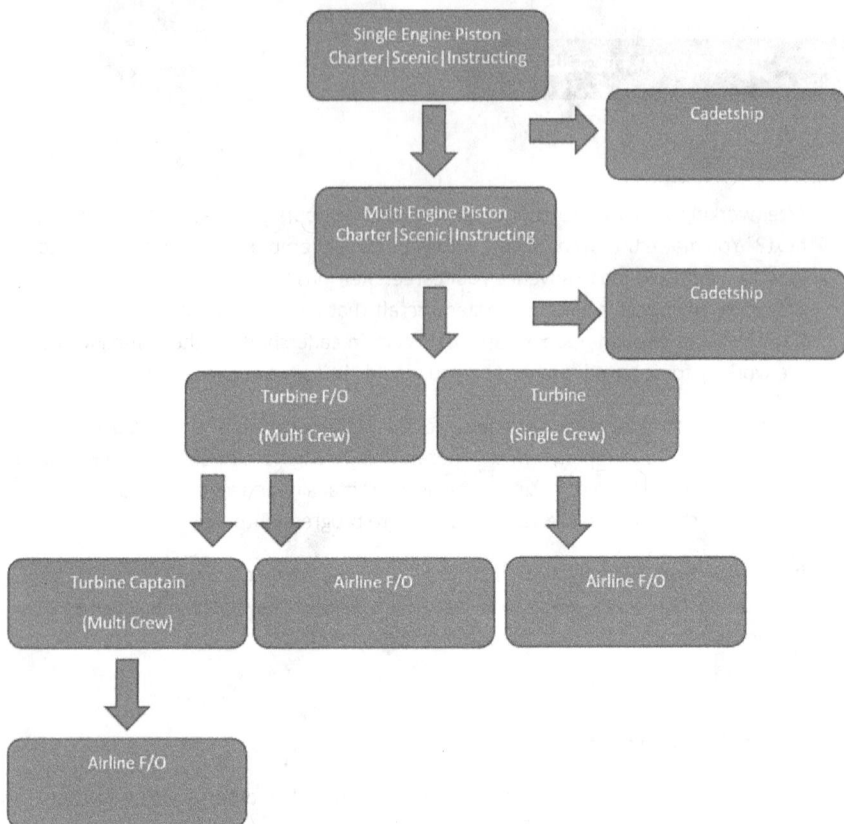

You could expect to fly a single engine piston aircraft before moving onto a multi-engine piston aircraft. From there you would potentially meet the minimum requirements for a direct entry First Officer position in the airlines, however because there is so much competition, most pilots find that the next step is to gain hours on a propeller turbine aircraft (whether multi or single crew). From there you may progress to he left hand seat as a Captain, move onto another turbine aircraft, or be accepted for an interview with an airline.

The list of opportunities and career paths to an airline is endless. Perhaps your final goal is not to fly a jet aircraft but to have a stable career flying turbine aircraft, or fly part time whilst running your own business.

How many hours do you need to get into an airline?

Provided you are applying for a direct entry First Officer position, most airlines within Australia have the following minimum requirements:

✈   1500 hours total

✈   500 hours multi engine

✈   100 hours night

✈   ATPL

✈   Turbine experience preferred

However with the recent pilot shortages, airlines are taking pilots with a lot less experience. A major airline whom operates 777's are currently hiring 777 Second Officers and ATR First Officer with only 500 hours total and only single engine experience.

Real life examples of how long it may take to get into an airline.

Many flying schools will tell you that once you complete your training, you will have all the qualifications necessary for an airline position. This is not untrue, however the hard reality is that it takes many years to reach the stage where you will meet the minimum requirements for the airlines.

Some people gain the required aeronautical experience for an airline quickly, whilst others progress through different jobs at a slower pace. It is best to be reasonable and realistic in your expectations of how long it will take you to accrue the amount of experience required by most airlines. The minimum requirements stated on an airlines website are also just that - the bare minimum. Although some airlines set out a minimum of say 1500 hours total and 500 hours on a multi-engine aircraft, some pilots with 3000 hours total have been unsuccessful in their applications due to being noncompetitive.

Throughout your journey, you may be able to accept cadetships into an airline as a First Officer. You should be aware however of the potential costs involved, and/or reduced training salary over a direct entry First Officer. You may also be "bonded" – that is provide a certain number of years of service for the company. If you leave before your bond has expired, you will be liable to pay the remainder of it pro rata.

On the following page are differing flow charts of real life examples of how long it has taken some pilots to progress through their career as a pilot.

The green box shows the year including those during flying training. Each box shows the job number, the type of flying and the flying hours when they started and when they finished.

PILOT 1	PILOT 2	PILOT 3
1st Year	Start Flying Training Ab Initio → CPL 0 – 150 hours	Start Flying Training Ab Initio → CPL 0 – 150 hours	Start Flying Training Ab Initio → CPL 0 – 200 hours
2nd Year	Finish Flying Training CPL → MECIR 150 -250 hours	Finish Flying Training CPL → MECIR 150 -200 hours	Finish Flying Training CPL → Instructor 200 -290 hours
3rd Year	First Job Single Engine Scenic 250 – 850 hours	First Job Single Engine Charter 200 – 500 hours	First Job Instructing Single Engine 290 - 810
4th Year	Second Job Multi Engine Charter 850 – 1400 hours	Second Job Multi Engine Charter Followed by Multi Crew, Turbine, Captain 500 – 2000 hours	Second Job Multi Engine Charter 810 – 1800 hours
5th Year	Third Job Widebody Second Officer 1400 - Present		Third Job Multi Crew, Large Turbine, F/O 1800 - 3100
6th Year		Third Job Jet Charter F/O 2000 - Present	Fourth Job Jet Airline F/O 3100 - Present
7th Year			
8th Year			
9th Year			

Life as an airline pilot

As you can see, life as an airline pilot comes with both the positive and negatives. Each airline also has different working conditions and pay scales defined by their individual *Enterprise Bargaining Agreements* (EBA).

Most airlines provide pilots with either a 28 or 56 day roster, with the next roster being published two weeks before the current one is to expire. Some airlines will allow pilots to bid for certain days off, trips and pairings. Airline work is shift work and pilots are required to flying at any time of the day or night, including holidays. As such, most pilots are given 6 weeks of annual leave per year in lieu of public holidays.

Airlines have to conform to the flight and duty limits laid out by CASA in the *Civil Aviation Orders* (CAO's) or fatigue management scheme that the airline has published in consultation with CASA. Airlines are normally restricted to rostering pilots for not more than 1000 hours flight time per year. Flight hour means from when the aircraft pushes back from the gate till arriving at the gate at the destination. This does not include the time since sign on for flight planning, ordering fuel and preflight checks. The duty time is the time from when a pilot signs on till signoff which is between 15-30 minutes after the flight arrives at the gate.

Most pilots are paid a base salary plus superannuation, overtime, day off payments and allowances. The overtime threshold is normally anywhere from 60-90 hours flying per month. Any flight hours accrued over the threshold are paid at the applicable rate. Whether overtime is paid to pilots however is dependent on that airlines specific EBA.

Pilots are normally given between 8-10 days off per month. Any days that are either not an RDO or a flight are reserve or standby days which means that the pilot must be contactable during that period and must be available to work if required. If a pilot decides to work on his or her day off they may receive a payment for working on such a day.

When a pilot flies to a destination and has to overnight at a port other than their home base, they will usually receive an allowance which covers the amount of money a pilot could reasonably expect to pay for food during the time spent away from home base. The company pays for the accommodation during the overnight.

Some airlines can move pilots to different bases through Australia depending on their needs whilst others have particular clauses in their EBAs stating that they may not move pilots during their employment unless mutually agreed upon.

Domestic airline pilots can expect to fly between one to five sectors each day that they are rostered. This depends on the airline and the length of the flights. International pilots normally fly longer sectors and thus less sectors and days per month.

The first position a pilot can expect to obtain in an airline is either as a Second Officer of a wide body jet (777or 787) or more likely as a First Officer of a narrow body jet (737, A320 or E-Jet). Most airlines operate a seniority system, whereby new positions and upgrade to Captain occur when the pilot is "next in line". That is, the first pilot to be employed by the company is given a seniority number of 1, the second 2 and so on. Progression to a Captain can take anywhere from 3-10 years depending on the company. That is, from when you start flying training to when you become a captain at an airline can take up to 12-20 years.

It can take quite a number of years to gain the experience required to apply for an airline, however once you are successful, being an airline pilot is a challenging yet very rewarding career. It is one of the most enviable careers available, where every day is different and the "office desk" is unlike any other.

With hard work and perseverance, this too can be your office

Boeing 737-800

Rosters

Your roster and how much you work per day and per month can vary greatly depending on which airline you fly for and which fleet or aircraft you are on. I have listed three different rosters on the following pages to show what a roster at an airline can look like. One is for regional flying such as on an ATR, Dash 8 or similar. The other is working on a 737, A320, E-Jet or similar, flying regular public transport domestically through Australia and the last is a roster for an international pilot flying a 777, 787 or similar. Note that that these are generic rosters which are designed to give you an idea off what a roster period in the life of an airline pilot can look like.

The following legend applies to these mock rosters:

✈	LOR	Layover at hotel
✈	RES	Reserve/on call
✈	RDO	Rostered day off
✈	OPEN	Reserve/on call
✈	PAX	"Passenger" to another airport to pickup a flight
✈	ADL	Adelaide
✈	AUH	Abu Dhabi
✈	BNE	Brisbane
✈	BUD	Bundaberg
✈	CNS	Cairns
✈	EML	Emerald
✈	GLT	Gladstone
✈	LAX	Los Angeles
✈	LCT	Launceston
✈	MCK	Mackay
✈	MEL	Melbourne
✈	PMQ	Port Macquarie
✈	PTH	Perth
✈	ROK	Rockhampton
✈	ROM	Roma
✈	SYD	Sydney

AUSTRALIAN AIRWAYS (REGIONAL)

ROSTER

PILOT: JOE BLOGGS

DAY	DUTY	SIGN ON	SIGN OFF	DETAILS	DUTY TIME	FLIGHT TIME	OVER NIGHT
Monday	RDO	-	-	ROSTERED DAY OFF	-	-	
Tuesday	FLY	1515	2130	BNE-GLT-ROK	06:20	04:00	YES
Wednesday	FLY	0850	1900	ROK-BNE-EMD-BNE	09:00	04:10	
Thursday	RES	0800	2000	RESERVE	-	-	
Friday	RDO	-	-	ROSTERED DAY OFF	-	-	
Saturday	RDO	-	-	ROSTERED DAY OFF	-	-	
Sunday	FLY	12:00	18:00	BNE-BUD-BNE-EML-BNE	08:30	05:20	
Monday	FLY	13:00	19:00	PAX SYD SYD-CBR-SYD-CBR	06:00	03:00	YES
Tuesday	FLY	06:00	14:50	CBR-SYD-PMQ-SYD-CBR	06:50	03:40	YES
Wednesday	FLY	06:30	15:40	CBR-MEL-CBR PAX BNE	09:10	04:30	
Thursday	FLY	04:35	08:50	BNE-MOV-BN	05:45	03:30	
Friday	FLY	06:05	10:30	BNE-ROK-BNE	04:40	02:55	
Saturday	RDO	-	-	ROSTERED DAY OFF	-	-	
Sunday	RDO	-	-	ROSTERED DAY OFF	-	-	
Monday	FLY	09:30	18:00	PAX MEL MEL-LCT-MEL	-	-	YES
Tuesday	FLY	07:30	15:30	MEL-CBR-SYD-PMQ-BNE	08:00	05:55	
Wednesday	FLY	1500	2100	BNE-GLT-ROK	06:00	04:00	YES
Thursday	FLY	0850	1900	ROK-BNE-EMD-BNE	09:00	04:00	
Friday	RES	08:00	18:00	RESERVE	-	-	
Saturday	RES	06:00	18:00	RESERVE	-	-	
Sunday	RDO	-	-	ROSTERED DAY OFF	-	-	
Monday	RDO	-	-	ROSTERED DAY OFF	-	-	
Tuesday	FLY	08:00	16:00	BNE-GLT-MCK-CNS	10:00	05:20	YES
Wednesday	FLY	07:50	13:50	CNS-MCK-GLT-BNE	07:00	05:10	
Thursday	FLY	11:55	16:00	BNE-ROM-BNE	04:05	03:05	
Friday	RDO	13:15	20:05	BNE-GLT-GLT-BNE-GLT	06:55	04:10	YES
Saturday	RDO	10:30	18:30	GLT-BNE-ROM-BNE	08:00	04:50	
Sunday	RES	08:00	18:00	RESERVE	-	-	

TOTALS

DUTY HOURS: 82.3

FLIGHT HOURS: 58.9

28 DAY ROSTER

AUSTRALIAN AIRWAYS (DOMESTIC)

ROSTER

PILOT: JOE BLOGGS

DAY	DUTY	SIGN ON	SIGN OFF	DETAILS	DUTY TIME	FLIGHT TIME	OVER NIGHT
Monday	RES	08:00	20:00	RESERVE	-	-	
Tuesday	FLY	05:00	13:30	SYD-CNS-SYD	03:05	02:50	
Wednesday	FLY	06:00	16:40	SYD-CNS-SYD-MEL	10:40	05:30	YES
Thursday	FLY	06:30	16:30	MEL-PTH-MEL-SYD	10:00	07:00	
Friday	FLY	11:00	19:30	SYD-BNE-SYD-BNE-SYD	08:30	05:55	
Saturday	RDO	-	-	ROSTERED DAY OFF	-	-	
Sunday	RDO	-	-	ROSTERED DAY OFF	-	-	
Monday	RDO	-	-	ROSTERED DAY OFF	-	-	
Tuesday	RES	11:00	20:00	RESERVE	-	-	
Wednesday	FLY	08:00	18:00	PAX BNE BNE-CNS-BNE-SYD	10:00	05:40	
Thursday	FLY	08:30	13:35	SYD-MEL-SYD-BNE	05:05	03:55	YES
Friday	FLY	07:30	14:00	BNE-ROK-BNE-SYD-MEL	06:30	04:50	YES
Saturday	FLY	05:30	09:05	MEL-SYD-MEL	04:05	02:40	YES
Sunday	FLY	06:00	08:50	MEL-SYD	02:50	01:20	
Monday	FLY	11:00	15:50	SYD-BNE-SYD	04:50	02:50	
Tuesday	RDO			ROSTERED DAY OFF			
Wednesday	FLY	09:00	18:30	SYD-ADL-PTH	09:30	06:00	YES
Thursday	FLY	08:30	17:50	PTH-ADL-SYD	09:20	05:50	
Friday	RES	06:30	18:30	RESERVE	-	-	
Saturday	RDO	-	-	ROSTERED DAY OFF	-	-	
Sunday	RDO	-	-	ROSTERED DAY OFF	-	-	
Monday	FLY	10:00	18:00	PAX BNE BNE-CNS-BNE-SYD	07:00	05:30	YES
Tuesday	RDO	-	-	ROSTERED DAY OFF	-	-	
Wednesday	RDO	-	-	ROSTERED DAY OFF	-	-	
Thursday	RES	08:00	12:00	RESERVE	-	-	
Friday	FLY	07:00	12:30	PAX BNE BNE-SYD	05:30	01:10	
Saturday	RDO	-	-	ROSTERED DAY OFF	-	-	
Sunday	RDO	-	-	ROSTERED DAY OFF	-	-	

TOTALS

DUTY HOURS: 96.9

FLIGHT HOURS: 61.0

28 DAY ROSTER

AUSTRALIAN AIRWAYS (INTERNATIONAL) ROSTER

PILOT: JOE BLOGGS

DAY	DUTY	SIGN ON	SIGN OFF	DETAILS	DUTY TIME	FLIGHT TIME	OVER NIGHT
Monday	RDO	-	-	ROSTERED DAY OFF	-	-	
Tuesday	FLY	08:00	05:00	BNE-LAX	15:00	13:00	YES
Wednesday	LOR	-	-	LAYOVER	-	-	YES
Thursday	LOR	-	-	LAYOVER	-	-	YES
Friday	FLY	21:00	→	LAX-BNE	16:00	13:00	
Saturday	FLY	→	→	LAX-BNE			
Sunday	FLY	→	06:00	LAX-BNE			
Monday	RDO	-	-	ROSTERED DAY OFF	-	-	
Tuesday	RDO	-	-	ROSTERED DAY OFF	-	-	
Wednesday	RDO	-	-	ROSTERED DAY OFF	-	-	
Thursday	RDO	-	-	ROSTERED DAY OFF	-	-	
Friday	RDO	-	-	ROSTERED DAY OFF	-	-	
Saturday	RDO	-	-	ROSTERED DAY OFF	-	-	
Sunday	RDO	-	-	ROSTERED DAY OFF	-	-	
Monday	OPEN	05:00	10:00	OPEN	05:00	-	
Tuesday	OPEN	05:00	10:00	OPEN	05:00	-	
Wednesday	OPEN	05:00	10:00	OPEN	05:00	-	
Thursday	FLY	16:00	18:50	PAX SYD	02:50	-	
Friday	FLY	08:00	23:30	SYD-AUH	14:30	13:00	YES
Saturday	LOR	-	-	LAYOVER	-	-	YES
Sunday	LOR	-	-	LAYOVER	-	-	YES
Monday	LOR	-	-	LAYOVER	-	-	YES
Tuesday	FLY	09:00	→	AUH-SYD	16:30	12:30	
Wednesday	FLY	→	13:30	AUH-SYD PAX SYD-BNE			
Thursday	RDO	-	-	ROSTERED DAY OFF	-	-	
Friday	RDO	-	-	ROSTERED DAY OFF	-	-	
Saturday	RDO	-	-	ROSTERED DAY OFF	-	-	
Sunday	OPEN	06:00	10:00	OPEN	04:00	-	

TOTALS

DUTY HOURS: 83.8

FLIGHT HOURS: 51.5

28 DAY ROSTER

How much can you expect to be paid as a pilot?

This depends on what aircraft you fly and the company you work for. When employed with smaller, general aviation companies, most pay is calculated based on the Government Award for the position. With larger companies including airlines which typically have unions, pay scales and conditions are based largely on Enterprise Bargaining Agreements or EBA's, which more closely align the needs of the pilots to what the actual work conditions are.

Below is a list of expected base salaries for differing jobs in the aviation industry. These salaries are base only and do not include overnight allowances, day off payments, overtime and any other payments such as retention bonuses etc that may be payable.

AIRCRAFT	POSITION	SALARY (Gross Annual)
Single engine piston	Charter or scenic	$30,000 - $38,000
Multi-engine piston	Charter or scenic	$38,000 - $50,000
Prop Turbine (less than 10T*)	First Officer	$45,000 - $55,000
Prop Turbine (less than 10T*)	Captain	$65,000 - $85,000
Prop Turbine (over 10T*)	First Officer	$60,000 - $80,000
Prop Turbine (over 10T*)	Captain	$100,000 - $140,000
Airline (737, A320 or similar)	First Officer	$90,000 - $130,000
Airline (737, A320 or similar)	Captain	$180,000 - $200,000
Airline (A330, 777 or similar)	Captain	$200,000 - $300,000

* Less than 10T means turbine aircraft which have a maximum weight of less than 10 tonnes. This applies to aircraft such as the Fairchild Metroliner, Beech King Air and Cessna Conquest.

Turbine aircraft above 10T refers to larger, high capacity operations such as the Dash 8, Dash 8-400 and ATR-72.

On top of base salaries for airline and large prop pilots, most companies pay overnight, overtime and check and training allowances. A pilot can expect to earn anywhere from $10,000-$30,000 additional per year from allowances and if they are employed as a check or training captain, an additional $10,000-$30,000 per year in addition to base salary.

As a guide, if you are employed with a major airline in Australia as a First or Second Officer, you can expect to be paid approximately $160-$200 a night whenever you are on a trip away from home (layover). If you are called in to work on a day off, you can expect to be paid anywhere from $450-$800 per day and overtime from about $80-$120 per hour.

EBA's and Awards

Most small aviation companies including positions as a pilot at your first flying job will be covered by a government award. The award is a document that works in conjunction with the National Employment Standards to provide rules surrounding a pilot's employment that covers both the employee and employer. The latest pilot award at the time of publishing was the *Air Pilots Award 2010*. This document can be found on the Fair Work Australia website as a PDF and I would highly recommend either printing or downloading it and uploading it your tablet for future reference. The award can be found at the following address and typing the word "pilot" in the award title search.

www.fwc.gov.au/awards-and-agreements/awards/find-award

For a list of EBA's relating specifically to pilots, you can search the Fair Work Australia website for any agreement lodged with the fair work commission. This can be found at the following address:

www.fwc.gov.au/awards-and-agreements/agreements/find-agreement

This chapter includes short stories on fellow pilot's careers - how they became interested in aviation, the challenges they have faced during their career and how they got to where they are today. By reading these stories you'll be able to see that there a number of different way to become a pilot. Either through the military or through civilian avenues such as a cadetship or building hours though either instructing, charter, scenic or survey operations.

Every pilot that has written these stories has had the same qualities – perseverance, a willingness to learn and to do anything it takes to achieve their dream of being a professional pilot.

No one I ever knew was I pilot; the thought of being a pilot hadn't even crossed my mind. That all changed whilst on school holidays, when at age 13 my grandma took me to a small country library, where I came across a promotional video for the Benalla Gliding Club. It explained what was involved in learning to fly gliders and most interestingly to me, there being no age limit to start (unlike powered flying) and you could go solo as early as age 15! As a child I always wanted to test myself by taking on responsibilities, and I saw this as the ultimate opportunity to do that.

For the remainder of the school holidays I dreamed of soaring around in the cloud tops, looking down from above with the freedom to go where ever I wanted. When I returned home to Adelaide, I was brought back to earth with the realisation that I had very little means of accessing flying training due the expense. As though it were meant to be, I attended a BBQ where I learned our family friend's son was in the Australian Air Force Cadets. After some research I was ecstatic to discover they offered, amongst other things, Air Force subsidised gliding courses to cadets in the School holidays. I signed up as soon as I was eligible, and became involved in gliding at the first opportunity. To pay for the lessons I flipped burgers at McDonalds (for $6.83 an hour) for a few hours each night after school, with the thought of soaring with eagles as my motivation.

At age 15, on my first Air cadet gliding camp, after about 8 hours of instruction in an old, wood and fabric motor glider, (called a Motorfalke, SF-25C if you want to Google it and have a laugh!) I went solo, and knew from then on that's what I wanted to do.

Two weeks after completing year 12, (where I studied subjects I thought would give me the best chance of being a pilot, English, Mathematics, Physics, Chemistry, Economics), while most of my mates were celebrating their new found freedom, working in pubs, partying and travelling, I went to work in the mines for 12 months to save for flight training (at the time, HECS loans were not available). I was very fortunate growing up, my parents offered to support me with training costs, however I was eager to get there under my own steam as best I could. I learned to fly at Air Gold Coast, where I undertook training by day and worked shift work at night to make ends meet. On weekends I would get up early and study theory and drive to Archerfield in Brisbane to sit the seemingly endless exams. 8 Months and 150 hours of flying later I gained my CPL. I went on to achieve my MECIR, and ATPL theory credits in the months that followed.

Getting a job was the next hurdle. There were, and always have been horror stories about the lengths pilots go to after completing training to obtain their first job. With those stories in mind I went about making myself as employable as possible, getting all the extras most employers will but often get overlooked by prospective pilots. A dangerous goods certificate (online course), a senior first aid certificate and all ATPL theory subjects. I then looked in the places I thought may get overlooked by pilots looking for their first job. I discovered through a friend who was flying out of Alice Springs at the time, an Aboriginal community that was home to a small community based airline on the edge of the Tanami Desert NT, called Lajamanu Air. I had an interview within a week and left home to start work in Lajamanu two days later.

I lived in an old renovated shed and flew Cessna 210's 206's and an Airvan, 6 days a week, to every place I'd never heard of, all over QLD, the NT and WA. 10 months and 800 Hours of flying later, I moved to Darwin to start a job with Hardy Aviation. I quickly progressed from single engine piston to multi engine, multi crew turbine gaining a command on the Metro shortly after turning 22. It was very exciting and challenging flying. During my time in Darwin I flew everything from freight, such as pearls, and crocodile eggs, helicopter engines and rotors to Dili in East Timor for CHC, scheduled passenger services, politicians, prisoners, miners, deported illegal fisherman to Kupang in Indonesia, sailors and their families to Ambon Indonesia, as well as government officials from Kota Sarong in West Papua.

After two years, and about 2800hrs flying experience I moved to Canberra to fly ATRs as a First Officer with Virgin Australia Regional Airlines. A year later I moved to Brisbane, before being offered an opportunity to work with Virgin Australia International as a Second Officer on the B777-300ER, flying long haul trips between *the USA, Australia and the Middle East. The rosters and lifestyle are fantastic, usually completing around five or six trips (of around 4 days duration) in any 56 day cycle. We spend a lot of time in the simulator, around once every 6 weeks to maintain our flying skills and theoretical knowledge, as well undertaking an annual Line Proficiency Assessment in the aircraft. The position of a Second Officer in long haul is largely managerial and decision making is a big focus, as appose to stick and rudder skills that were the forefront in my previous jobs. We enjoy a reasonable amount of down time which allows us to recuperate between trips. For myself, along with the fantastic staff travel benefits, I see it as an opportunity to catch up on all the travel I didn't have the time for as a career driven school leaver. Some of my work colleagues run small businesses on the side or pursue other interests, others simply prefer to spend time with family.*

If you have an interest in flying, but have any doubt whatsoever about the commitment it takes to make a career as a pilot, I would encourage you to take up flying. It is incredibly rewarding, although perhaps consider it as a recreation rather than as a career. Only a small percentage of pilots who go and spend the $100,000 needed to complete a CPL are determined enough to endure the trials and tribulations of getting to where they want to be, and go on to have a lasting career in aviation. Having said that, achieving success in aviation, is in my opinion, 80% attitude and 20% aptitude and skill.

If you have read through Robbie's book, by now you would have a good idea about the realities of what the road to becoming a career pilot is all about. If you are certain that you want to make a career of flying, grab onto it with both hands and give it everything you've got. If you do it for the right reasons and have a genuine passion for flying, you will never truly work a day in your life.

John Tilley

At 4 years old my father took me to an airshow and I spent much of the day on his shoulders, looking up at planes zooming past and from that day forward I was hooked. I spent my high school years picking subjects which would allow me to pursue my career goals and was fortunate enough to have the odd flying lesson during school holidays in the later years of high school. After Year 12, I gained placement at the University of New South Wales where I completed my degree in Aviation and gained my Commercial Pilots Licence.

My first job was as a voluntary instructor with the Australian Air Force Cadets at Camden during school holidays. Soon after this, I was employed as a full time flying and theory instructor at Bankstown Airport where I taught cadet pilots from international airlines including India, Japan and Malaysia. Having spent a number of years building my hours I decided it was time to leave the instructing scene and look for other work to enhance my skills and experience. I left Sydney looking for charter work on bigger aircraft. Initially this proved to be a very slow and almost fruitless process. However the odd job here and there kept my head above water.

Eventually my lucky break came when I scored a job flying freight and charter contracts on a Saab 340. My first multi-crew and turbine job! After a number of years flying "back of the clock" the regional airlines in Australia started hiring again and I was able to get a job with a major airline flying RPT as a First Officer.

Salah Bahmad

I was one of those kids that always wanted to fly. My earliest memory is of watching the RPT Chieftains landing at the local aerodrome. Later I was watching the aeromedical King Air's, and from then on that's all I ever wanted to do. When I was 14 I completed a Trial Instructional Flight at my local aero club in country Victoria and went solo shortly after my 16th birthday. I completed my CPL when I was 18 years of age when I was in Year 12. Instead of studying text books for my Year 12 exams I would be reading flying books. As soon as school finished I was working at the local aero club flying charter and scenics. From here I made the big move to the Northern Territory as many young pilots do and there was no looking back. I then flew for two charter companies in my time, flying Cessna 206, 210's, Barons and Caravans. I had a brief interlude at this point, moving back to Victoria before moving cross country again, this time to live in Derby, WA. I was back flying Cessna Caravan's out to remote stations and communities delivering the mail and operating crew changes to an iron ore mine on the Kimberley coast.

I then followed my girlfriend who was also a pilot to Darwin, taking a position as a First Officer on a Fairchild Metroliner. My job primarily entailed flying personnel employed in oil, gas and the resource industry to Truscott in Western Australia and The Granites in the Tanami Desert. I spent six months as a First Officer before being offered the opportunity to become a Captain. The chance to be a Captain of a turboprop in multi-crew operations was a great experience and one which honed my skills as a professional pilot.

At the beginning of 2013 my ambition to move into an aeromedical role was realised and I embarked on my journey as a pilot flying a Beechcraft King Air with CareFlight in Darwin. This is a role I enjoy every day and the variety and challenge of flying single pilot IFR in this environment is unrivalled in my career so far. I now lead a talented team of pilots in my role as Senior Base Pilot and thoroughly enjoy training new pilots in air ambulance operations in the Northern Territory.

The experience that I gained as a fresh commercial pilot in remote Northern Territory flying a Cessna 210 has been invaluable. I have been able to carry these experiences with me each and every day into my career and I am very grateful for the guidance and advice from my mentors along the way.

Matthew Mommers

Ever since I can remember, I have always wanted to fly. I remember finishing school and thinking how can I pull this off with no money and no direct support.

So begins the journey. The battle of achieving a goal and starting right at the very bottom. It all starts with a little motivation and perseverance.

I was working at McDonalds at the time saving up for a course that could pay well. I worked three jobs while studying for my travel degree working all different hours of the day, seven days a week. I achieved my certificate and within a month I obtained my first job at a travel company working as a consolidator earning a good salary which in turn went directly into my "flying account". I worked in that job for two and a half years and then obtained a position with Qantas at Melbourne airport which was a fantastic job. It gave me the flexibility to work various shifts so I could head down to Moorabbin airport and start learning to fly.

After 3 years at Qantas I earned my private pilot licence as well as my commercial pilot licence with a night rating and multi-engine endorsement. I decided to start job hunting using my staff travel flights to travel around the country dropping off resumes and in the process look for my first charter gig.

After no success in the first couple of months, I decided to take the step and leave my well paying job at Qantas to move to Darwin to wait and hope for a job to come soon. In the mean time I worked for a regional airline in a ground based role for a few months before I was offered a check ride with a small charter company based in Darwin. It went well and I was offered a casual position flying scenic and charter flights. After a few more months that turned into a full time position. Along the way I've made some great friends and also shared many experiences.

My advice to anyone looking at becoming a pilot is to work hard and never give up.

Etienne Muscat

Going through a cadetship was a completely unexpected but incredible experience. I've been exposed to aviation all my life as my father is also a pilot and growing up, many of my fondest memories of family holidays were the flight to and from the destination. It took me a long time to realise it was a career path I could also go down but after my first trial flight I couldn't imagine doing anything else.

I initially started my own path into aviation through a university degree which in itself was a fantastic experience and formed friendships with people from all different back grounds working toward a multitude of varying avenues in flying and aviation management.

After successfully applying for the cadetship, the following years were a blur of training. My course mates and instructors were exceptionally and uniquely talented and I am so grateful for their help throughout the course. One of the greatest challenges was learning balance, working and studying hard is important but knowing when to rest and take some time out to recuperate was critical to avoid burning out.

Coming into flying full time was extremely challenging but also more rewarding than I could have ever imagined. As a cadet you do have very limited experience so every day at work I try and learn from the vast experience of the crew. One of the things I love is that you can keep pushing yourself to improve whether flying on the line or in the sim, not to mention the incredible views along the way.

The people I have met and the beautiful places seen along the way that I'll never forget have already made it an unforgettable experience and I look forward to wherever the futures ends up taking me.

Elle France

My aviation journey began on a Qantas 747-400 at the age of four months and by the time I commenced flying training at 15 years old, I had been fortunate enough to spend enough time in and around the aviation environment that the flying bug had been well and truly entrenched in my blood. I went solo shortly after my 16th birthday and continued to train part time at Bankstown Airport until I moved to Melbourne and commenced the Swinburne Aviation Tafe flying program. This program expedited my training and meant I was fully qualified to venture down the general aviation path in just under two years with the view to joining an airline down the track.

As everyone will tell you, networking in aviation is your best friend and my biggest stroke of luck came about when I found my first job in general aviation as a result of some fortuitous timing and sheer good luck. I had completed an ATPL theory course at the Sunshine Coast and was driving back to Sydney with a friend when I decided to drop into Ballina Airport where I had completed a small amount of flying training several years earlier. By chance, I came across the same instructor I had flown with and he remembered me when I told him my name and he recognized it by virtue of having it in his logbook. He couldn't help me out with a job, but pointed me in the direction of the owner/chief pilot of a small start-up company next door. We had a chat and he showed me around his aircraft – an immaculate 1966 Twin Comanche. We exchanged details and less than six months later, an email came through out of the blue suggesting that he may need a pilot. All of the cards fell in my favour and soon after I was given two days to move up, get settled and commence whale watching scenic charters in his Twin Comanche off the coast of Northern NSW – it wasn't a bad first job!

Having now worked for several companies within the industry and flown a variety of aircraft in several different types of operations, including skydiving, freight runs and fly-in fly-out, I have gained an amazing amount of life experience to go along with the thousands of hours I have accumulated in the air.

The challenges that you can expect to face going down this path can be both varied and overwhelming in their nature at times but flexibility, a cool head and thoroughly understanding expectations from each side of the coin will help you move through the inevitable obstacles that you will find in your way from time to time.

Networking can again help you to move through these obstacles as the more people that you know in the industry, the more experiences you can draw on to help you navigate the often complicated path of general aviation. Talk to and get to know as many people in as many corners of the industry as you can because you never know when you might just need a different opinion, whether it's in the air or on the ground. Passion for aviation is a common trait amongst pilots so it will never be hard to strike up a conversation with someone on an apron or in a terminal and you never know where that will lead.

Going forward, I have spent four and a half years in general aviation and the numerous challenges, difficulties and incredible experiences have stood me in good stead for the next stage of my career that will commence shortly with a major international airline.

Sam Vielie

Conclusion

I hope that this book has been able to give you an insight into the world of aviation and has answered some questions you may have had, from deciding if you want to fly, all the way through to what to do after you have gained the experience to move onto greater things. I also hope that you have learnt some valuable tips, so that you can avoid the common traps and pitfalls associated with aviation.

Keeping a diary

Many of my fellow pilot friends, myself included, wish that we had kept a journal or diary during our time in general aviation. Every airline pilot I speak to says that the best job they had was those in general aviation when they were actually flying the plane; hands on.

You will look back on your first job with fond memories. If you keep a journal during your career, you can jot down the things that went wrong and the important lessons learnt, events that occurred during your flying, the people you have met or a particular thing that someone said.

Photos

Take as many photos as you can! Nowadays all phones have great cameras that can take pictures of all the amazing experiences you will encounter throughout your aviation journey. You will look back on your photos with fond memories. Just remember that you're in general aviation and your first job in the outback for a good time, not a long time.

Despite all the photos for this book having been taken on my phone, I have since delved more into photograph and wish that I had a decent camera during my time building up hours. If you are really into your photography, I would recommend biting the bullet and purchasing a DSLR camera, if you have the money to afford one once you have finished your training. There are some amazing sunrises, sunsets and landscapes to see in the middle of Australia and the closest way to appreciate them apart from being there is with an incredible photo.

If you need any further information, there are many websites and forums that you may find useful, listed below.

1)   www.pprune.org

A forum, worldwide with a large Australian presence, right through from air traffic controllers, people learning to fly and Captains of jet aircraft. Once you head to their homepage you will want to click on the link "The Pacific: General Aviation & Questions". If you create an account you can search the site and also post your own threads. Be wary of the information contained on this website as it does contain the opinions of people rather than hard facts.

2)   www.casa.gov.au

The Civil Aviation Safety Authority website contains not only information on learning to fly but also a myriad of other information and pilot guides that can be useful during flight training. If you are learning to fly at Parafield airport, Jandakot airport, Archerfield airport, or in the Melbourne or Sydney area, their Visual pilot guides are definitely worth downloading.

Also useful is the visual flight rules guide, which is a simple and easy to read guide with all rules, regulations and information required for a VFR pilot. The airport and VFR pilot guides can be found at the CASA website then selecting the "education" tab from the top and selecting the appropriate manual.

3)   www.airservicesaustralia.com

Airservices Australia is the corporate company providing air traffic control services through Australia as well as weather and NOTAM information for pilots. Electronic copies of the ERSA, DAP and AIP can be found on their website under the publications tab.

Key points to remember

Below I have compiled a list of the most common pitfalls that can cost you either time or money during your training and flying career. If you only remember a few things from this book, remember the points below:

✈ Before starting flying training make sure that you are medically fit and obtain an ARN and medical.

✈ Choose a reputable flying school and ask as many questions as you can. A detailed list of potential questions to ask can be found in chapter 4.

✈ A flying school that offers integrated courses allows a pilot to complete their CPL in a minimum of 150 hours, rather than the normal 200.

✈ Remember that schools can charge on either VDO or airswitch time.

✈ Deciding which avenue you take to build your hours, either an instructor rating or instrument rating (and then where to find a job and of what type) is a very important decision.

✈ As a charter pilot you need a dangerous good awareness certificate. You also need a current Class 1 medical.

✈ On average, the hardest requirement to accrue for the ATPL licence is the 100 hours night. If you have any chances during you flying training to do navigation exercises at night or when you have a job and are doing a drop off late in the afternoon and are able to sit on the ground till nightfall to accrue hours, do it.

✈ Network as much as you can and talk to as many people as possible.

This chapter contains valuable information specifically for international students studying flying training within Australia. Many flying schools in Australia cater flying training tailored towards the needs of international students, whether completing a licence as an individual or through an approved course as an employee of an overseas airline.

Entry Requirements

To learn to fly in Australia, CASA sets out a minimum standard of english language proficiency. There are three english tests that that CASA has nominated as acceptable to be able to study in Australia. These are IELTS, TOEFL and TOEIC. If english is not your first language than you must have a minimum IELTS score of 5.5.

More information can be found on the CASA website at the following address:

www.casa.gov.au/standard-page/general-english-test-criteria

Visa

The government, through the *Department of Immigration and Border Protection* (DIBP) allows students to enter Australia to study on many different visas. The visa most commonly used by approved flight schools is the *Vocational Education and Training Sector* visa (subclass 572). The requirement for a 572 class visa is that you are enrolled as a student in a registered vocational education and training course.

There are two ways of applying for a 572 visa. The first is directly through the flying school you wish to train with. They may do this for you or alternatively they may email you a form which you will need to complete. The second method is through an agent. Details for agents may be found by contacting the flying school directly.

If you are successful in obtaining a visa, you will be given a letter of offer. You must sign this letter and send the offer of acceptance back to the flying school. This can usually be done via mail, email or facsimile. After you have accepted the offer you will need to pay a deposit and you will then receive an email of confirmation of enrolment.

Overseas Student Health Cover

Australia provides health cover for international students under *the Overseas Student Health Cover* (OSHC). When studying in Australia, you will need OSHC for yourself, and any family travelling with you, before you arrive. It is a requirement of your student visa that you maintain OSHC for the duration of your time on a student visa in Australia. The OSHC can help you pay for medical or hospital care you may need while you're studying in Australia.

OSHC is a mandatory insurance cover that may either be obtained directly through the flying school or through an insurer website that provides OSHC. The following companies provide OSHC in Australia:

✈ *Australian Health Management* www.ahmoshc.com
✈ *BUPA Australia* www.bupa.com.au/health-insurance/cover/oshc
✈ *Medibank Private* www.medibank.com.au/oshc
✈ *Allianz Global Assistance* www.oshcallianzassistance.com.au
✈ *NIB* www.nib.com.au/overseas-students

More information about the health cover can be found on the department of health website and searching for "Overseas Student Health Cover"
http://www.health.gov.au/

Planning your departure

Once you have been accepted to start flying training in Australia, you should consider the following before you leave home:

```
┌─────────────────────┐
│  Current Passport and │
│         Visa          │
└─────────────────────┘
           │
           ▼
┌─────────────────────┐
│    Taken out OSHC     │
└─────────────────────┘
           │
           ▼
┌─────────────────────┐        ┌───────────────────────────────┐
│    Travel Insurance   │  ─ ─> │ OSHC  only  covers  medical   │
└─────────────────────┘        │ implications. Travel insurance can │
                               │ cover things such as flight delays, │
                               │ missing luggage, theft, additional │
                               │ medical and dental care.      │
                               └───────────────────────────────┘
```

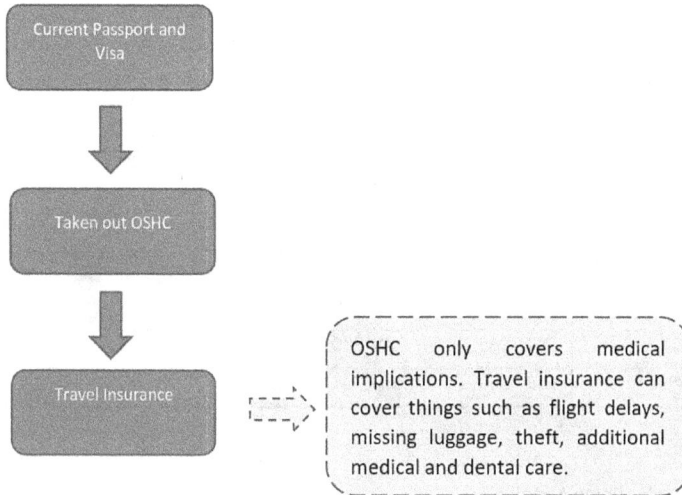

The Australian Government also provides a lot of generic information for anyone who would like to study in Australia. Information includes topics on why to study in Australia, facts and figures, visa and entry requirements, planning your departure, living costs and general life in Australia. Further information can be found on their website at the following address: www.studyinaustralia.gov.au

Arriving in Australia

When you arrive in Australia, the first thing you will have to do is clear customs. Australia has strict custom and biosecurity laws that keep many pests and unwanted diseases out of Australia. You will be given an *Incoming Passenger Card* on your flight to Australia which you must fill out truthfully. There are many yes and no questions that you must answer on the front of the card.

Many items are illegal to bring into Australia. Some other items are also allowed, however they must be declared. One example is that if you are carry more than $10,000 worth of Australian currency into the country this must be declared on your incoming passenger card. Fresh fruit and vegetables, meat, poultry, pork, eggs, nuts, dairy goods and live plants and seeds are not allowed into the country and should be brought into Australia. Heavy fines can apply if you are caught bringing the above plant and animal materials in Australia.

How to get from the airport to the city,

If you are catching an international flight to Australia, chances are that you will be arriving in either Sydney, Melbourne or Brisbane. Below is a list of all different types of transportation options within Australia including taxis, Uber X, trains and busses.

The following table shows which type of transportation options are available from which airport and the approximate cost from the airport to the city center.

	TAXI	UBER	TRAIN	BUS
SYDNEY	$30 - $50	$30 - $70	$18	
MELBOURNE	$40 - $65	$40 - $80		$18
BRISBANE	$40 - $60	$30 - $45	$27	

Foreign Embassies in Australia

Foreign embassies and consulates are normally located in Canberra, ATC; the capital of Australia. Contact information for your specific embassy in Australia can be found at the following address:

www.protocol.dfat.gov.au/Consulate/list.rails

Overseas Students Ombudsman

If you have a complaint or dispute with your flying school you should first approach the school and address your concerns. If they are unable or unwilling to help you, you can apply for help via the *Overseas Students Ombudsman* (OSO). This is a free service for international visa students. More information about the Ombudsman can be found at the following address:

www.oso.gov.au

Mobile Phones and SIMs

There are three main providers of telecommunication and mobile plans within Australia. These are *Telstra, Optus* and *Vodafone.* These three companies also supply plans to other companies which piggybacking their infrastructures including mobile companies such as *Virgin Mobile, Amaysim, Boost, Vaya* and many more.

In Australia you may provide your own mobile phone and obtain a SIM card on either a plan or prepaid option, or you may sign up for a plan with a phone handset included. To compare mobile phone plans in Australia, two excellent websites are the following:

www.youcompare.com.au/mobilephones

www.whistleout.com.au/MobilePhones

Banking

Australia has a range of banking options. You may be able to set up a bank account before you arrive in Australia. To open a bank account in Australia you will need your Passport, email containing confirmation of enrolment at your flying school and another form of identification (usually at least 100 points of identification). In Australia, money can be deposited and withdrawn via a bank branch, an ATM (automatic teller machine) and some large stores including supermarkets. You are also able to access your bank account via telephone and internet banking.

You may be able to transfer money from your home account to your new Australian bank account. Fees and services depend on which bank you open an account with. A comparison tool for banks within Australia can be found at the following address:

www.oshc-compare.com.au/australian-bank-accounts

Aeronautical experience requirements

PRIVATE PILOTS LICENCE

- ✈ At least 17 years of age
- ✈ Learn the required theory
- ✈ Complete relevant flight training through a flying school
- ✈ Pass a PPL theory exam
- ✈ Pass a PPL flight test for the licence and category rating
- ✈ Meet the minimum aeronautical experience requirements stated below

INTEGRATED COURSE
>   35 hours aeronautical experience that includes:
>   30 hours flight time
>   10 hours of solo flight time
>   5 hours of solo cross country time
>   2 hours of dual instrument time

NON- INTEGRATED COURSE
>   40 hours aeronautical experience that includes:
>   35 hours flight time
>   10 hours of solo flight time
>   5 hours of solo cross country time
>   2 hours of dual instrument time

COMMERCIAL PILOTS LICENCE

✈ At least 18 years of age
✈ Learn the required theory
✈ Complete the relevant flight training through a flying school
✈ Pass the CPL theory examinations
✈ Meet the minimum aeronautical experience requirements (see below for more information)
✈ Pass a CPL flight test for the licence and category rating
✈ Meet the minimum aeronautical experience requirements stated below

INTEGRATED COURSE
150 hours aeronautical experience that includes:
140 hours flight time
70 hours as PIC
20 hours of cross country time
10 hours of instrument time

NON-INTEGRATED COURSE
200 hours aeronautical experience that includes:
190 hours flight time
100 hours as PIC
20 hours of cross country time
10 hours of instrument time

✈ At least 21 years of age
✈ Hold either a commercial pilot licence or multi-crew pilot licence with the same aircraft category rating
✈ Complete the relevant flight training through a flying school
✈ Pass the ATPL theory examinations
✈ Complete an approved course of multi-crew cooperation training
✈ Pass a ATPL flight test
✈ Meet the minimum aeronautical experience requirements stated below

INTEGRATED COURSE

	1400 hours aeronautical experience
	1500 flight time as pilot
	750 hours as PIC
Either	500 hours ICUS
Or	250 hours as PIC or ICUS with 70 hours being PIC
	200 hours of cross country time
	100 hours of cross country time as PIC or ICUS
	100 hours of night excluding dual
	75 hours of instrument time
	45 hours of instrument time in an aircraft (no sim)

Training airport facilities and locality

Most main airports that students learn to fly at are located near a capital city. These are normally the 'secondary' airports associated with each capital city which were originally designated as *GAAP* training areas but have now be reclassified as *Class D* aerodromes. The following information shows what transport and services are around the vicinity of each aerodrome you may be based at.

Archerfield, Brisbane

Archerfield aerodrome is approximately 10km south from Brisbane city. It services many flying school as well as smaller charter and freight companies. Getting to and from Archerfield is quite easy with busses running regularly to a bus stop outside the Eastern boundary of the aerodrome. Bus numbers 110 and 115 run direct from the airport to the city. The busses are run by *Translink* and timetables and scheduling are available through Google Maps or the Translink website at www.translink.com.au.

Archerfield contains an on field cafeteria for food during the day. The closest shopping center to Archerfield is *Acacia Marketplace* with *Sunnybank Plaza*; a larger shopping precinct, approximately 3km to the East.

Bankstown, Sydney

Bankstown aerodrome services the Sydney area, and is approximately 18km west of the city center. Bus and train is the easiest way to get to the airport with the T3 line running directly from the city to the Bankstown train station and the 905 bus running from there to the airport. Transport in Sydney is run through *Transport NSW*, timetables scheduling is available through Google Maps or their website at www.transportnsw.info.

Food is available at the aerodrome with the closest shopping center to Bankstown being the *Bankstown Centro* located in Bankstown city center.

Jandakot, Perth

Jandakot airport is located approximately 18km south of Perth. It is serviced from the city via trains on the Mandurah line. Trains are run by *Transperth* with timetables available from the following website: www.transperth.wa.gov.au.

Aviators Café, *Francesco's Cafe & Bar*, *Muzz Buzz* are cafes located on the aerodrome precinct with the closest groceries available at the airport from *Spud Shed*.

Moorabbin, Melbourne

Moorabbin airport is located approximately 24km to the south east of Melbourne. Moorabbin is accessed by trains from the city, with an interchange required at Richmond station. Journeys can be planned through the *Public Transport Victoria* website at www.ptv.vic.gov.au (note: Google maps does not show public transport in Melbourne). DFO Moorabbin is located on the airport precinct and contains two food courts.

Parafield, Adelaide

Parafield airport is located approximately 20km north of Adelaide. Parafield is accessed by train from the city on the GAWC line and takes approximately 40 minutes. *Adelaide Metro* runs the public transport in South Australia and their website is located at: www.adelaidemetro.com.au with train schedules available online or via Google maps.

Parafield Plaza Shopping Center is the nearest store and located to the west of the airport.

GLOSSARY

ADF	Australian Defence Force
ADFA	Australian Defence Force Academy
ADS-B	Automatic Dependent Surveillance Broadcast
AIP	Aeronautical Information Publication
AFAP	Australian Federation Air Pilots
ASA	Air Services Australia
ATSB	Air Transport Safety Bureau
BAK	Basic Aeronautical Knowledge (theory examination)
CASA	Civil Aviation Safety Authority
CPL	Commercial Pilot Licence
DAME	Designated aviation medical examiner
DAP	Departure and approach procedures
DUAL	hire of an aircraft with an instructor on board
EFB	Electronic Flight Bag
ERSA	En-route Supplement Australia
IATA	International Air Transport Association
ICAO	International Civil Aviation Organization
ICUS	In command under supervision
IFR	Instrument flight rules
IMC	Instrument meteorological conditions
IR	Instructor rating
IREX	Instrument rating examination
MECIR	Multi engine command instrument rating
NAV	Navigation
NOTAM	Notice to airmen
NVFR	Night visual flight rules
PIC	Pilot in command
PPL	Private Pilot Licence
RG	Retractable gear
RPL	Recreational Pilots Licence
SPL	Student Pilots Licence
VFR	Visual flight rules
VMC	Visual meteorological condition

PHONETIC ALPHABET

A	Alpha
B	Bravo
C	Charlie
D	Delta
E	Echo
F	Foxtrot
G	Golf
H	Hotel
I	India
J	Juliet
K	Kilo
L	Lima
M	Mike
N	November
O	Oscar
P	Papa
Q	Quebec
R	Romeo
S	Sierra
T	Tango
U	Uniform
V	Victor
W	Whiskey
X	X-ray
Y	Yankee
Z	Zulu

1	Wun
2	Too
3	Tree
4	Fow-er
5	Fife
6	Six
7	Sev-en
8	Ait
9	Niner
0	Ze-ro

www.ingramcontent.com/pod-product-compliance
Lightning Source LLC
Chambersburg PA
CBHW070250290326
41930CB00041B/2429